Reaching Standards
and Beyond
in Kindergarten

This book is dedicated to all young children, their families, and teachers with our fervent wish that their sense of wonder will spark a joy in learning that will blaze in their hearts for a lifetime.

Reaching Standards and Beyond in Kindergarten

Nurturing Children's Sense of Wonder and Joy in Learning

Gera Jacobs

··········

Kathy Crowley

A JOINT PUBLICATION

naeyc®

CORWIN
A SAGE Company

For information:

Corwin
A SAGE Company
2455 Teller Road
Thousand Oaks, California 91320
(800) 233-9936
Fax: (800) 417-2466
www.corwinpress.com

SAGE India Pvt. Ltd.
B 1/I 1 Mohan Cooperative
   Industrial Area
Mathura Road, New Delhi 110 044
India

SAGE Ltd.
1 Oliver's Yard
55 City Road
London EC1Y 1SP
United Kingdom

SAGE Asia-Pacific Pte. Ltd.
33 Pekin Street #02-01
Far East Square
Singapore 048763

Printed in the United States of America

Library of Congress Cataloging-in-Publication Data

Jacobs, Gera.
Reaching standards and beyond in kindergarten : nurturing children's sense of wonder and joy in learning/Gera Jacobs, Kathy Crowley.
      p. cm.
Includes bibliographical references and index.
ISBN 978-1-4129-5724-3 (cloth)
ISBN 978-1-4129-5725-0 (pbk.)
   1. Early childhood education—Activity programs. 2. Creative activities and seat work.
3. Play. I. Crowley, Kathy. II. Title.

LB1139.35.A37J365 2010
372.21'8—dc22   2009028203

This book is printed on acid-free paper.

09   10   11   12   13   10   9   8   7   6   5   4   3   2   1

Acquisitions Editor:	Jessica Allan
Editorial Assistant:	Joanna Coelho
Production Editor:	Amy Schroller
Copy Editor:	Tomara Kafka
Typesetter:	C&M Digitals (P) Ltd.
Proofreader:	Charlotte J. Waisner
Cover Designer:	Rose Storey

Contents

Preface

The focus of this book is on providing resources and ideas to help children reach national and state content standards in developmentally appropriate ways. Standards are only part of the picture; there is much more that we wish for our children. The book also offers suggestions for helping children reach beyond the standards to acquire good social skills, a strong sense of self-worth, and positive approaches to learning that will serve as a foundation for future learning. Although written primarily for kindergarten, these ideas can be used in preschool and the primary grades by adjusting the level of challenge.

Standards are a major component of education today. In this era of accountability, standards are often used as benchmarks to assess children's progress. Many teachers have felt the pressure of a "pushed down curriculum" and are concerned that children in kindergarten are inappropriately expected to do things that used to be required of older students. Teachers and administrators are searching for ways they can be accountable and help children reach standards, while still maintaining a developmentally appropriate classroom that allows children to play and still *be children*. They also need to know current research and how to share this information with parents. This book provides concrete research-based ideas and strategies teachers and administrators can use to answer these concerns. It provides background research in reader-friendly, understandable terms. The book brings fresh ideas to the kindergarten field that can provide first-year kindergarten teachers with strategies they need to have a successful year and veteran teachers reassurance about the good practices they are using, as well as suggestions to add to their repertoire. The book is designed for both preservice and inservice teachers, administrators, and all who are interested in working with children in this most important springtime of their lives.

There were many resources used in preparing this book. A key source was *Developmentally Appropriate Practices in Early Childhood Programs*, revised in 2009 by the National Association for the Education of Young Children. Their book, *K Today: Teaching and Learning in the Kindergarten Year* (Gullo, 2006) was another valuable resource. The Classroom Assessment Scoring System (CLASS) developed by the Center for the Advanced Study of Teaching and Learning provided additional insight into research-based practices. We reviewed national content standards written by the professional organizations, examined the compendium of standards and benchmarks developed by the Mid-continent Research for Education and Learning, and read through many of the individual state content standards as well. The design of national content standards differs widely. Some are written very broadly for K–12, such as those written by the International Reading Association and the National Council of Teachers of English. Several are divided into bands such as K–4, 5–8, and 9–12, while still others are broken down for specific grade levels, including mathematics, which also has curriculum focal points for specific grades. States also differ in the way their standards are organized and the areas included. In order to best serve their children, teachers need to be familiar with the state, national, or other standards expected of them. The ideas in this book provide suggestions that will help in this broad range of standards.

Chapter 1 provides an overview of the kindergarten year, including the origins of the first kindergarten and its purpose. The chapter deals with the importance and power of play, developing reciprocal relationships with families, and supporting the transition to kindergarten.

Chapter 2 describes how to set up a welcoming environment that facilitates children's learning. It also includes sample schedules for both full-day and half-day kindergartens.

Chapter 3 provides an introduction to engaging studies and projects as one way to help children meet standards in all areas of the curriculum. The chapter introduces ideas for authentically assessing children in developmentally appropriate ways, including observation, checklists, and portfolios.

Chapters 4 through 9 present ideas for helping children reach standards in all areas of the curriculum. The chapters contain suggestions for designing the environment and engaging experiences and studies that will help children meet standards. Each chapter also includes ideas for supporting children who are learning English as a new language and working with children's individual needs, including children with learning challenges, as well as those who have already mastered concepts. This group of chapters concludes in Chapter 9 with suggestions for social and emotional development and approaches to learning. Although most states do not include separate kindergarten standards for social and emotional development or approaches to learning, we know that much of children's learning is dependent on these areas.

Chapter 10 helps to connect the dots by tying concepts together and addressing issues of readiness, length of the kindergarten day, and the transition to first grade. The chapter ends with a list of goals for our children that will help them reach beyond the standards on the road to becoming concerned, active participants of their families, classrooms, and communities.

The chapters include *Try This!* suggestions with new ideas for helping children meet standards. There are also *Opportunities for Authentic Assessment* that offer added insight into using developmentally appropriate ways to track children's progress toward meeting the standards.

The Resource section contains a calendar that can be shared with families each month from August of the kindergarten year through the summer before first grade. The calendar includes daily suggestions for helping children reach standards through simple activities that are also designed to build parent-child relationships.

We hope that this book will provide a resource to advocate for the best possible developmentally appropriate kindergartens and standards for children. Our goal is that the ideas in this book will help support children's learning and development, while also nurturing their sense of wonder and joy in learning for a lifetime.

Acknowledgments

In the process of working on this project, we have come to the belief that it also takes a village to produce a book. This effort was truly a labor of love and not just on our part. We were blessed by the support of our families who offered encouragement, feedback, and suggestions. They kept the home fires burning and even managed to create time for us by taking on tasks to free us, including shopping and chauffeuring, so we could even write in the car! We would like to acknowledge our administrators: Gary Zalud, Rick Melmer, Darla Hamm, and Rosanne Yost for their support, and special thanks to Linda Reetz who also reviewed the book and offered insightful suggestions, as well as Diane Lowery and Deb Barnett from the South Dakota Department of Education. We would like to express our appreciation to others who took the time to carefully review the manuscript and provide helpful comments: Harriet Egertson, Carmen Stewart, Lacee Mills, June Holoch, Faith Tieszen, Darcy Sammelson, Sue Parrott, Wanda McKittrick, Jacqueline Jerke, Lucy Vandersnick, Lindy Obach, Katie Jacobs, Patty Crowley, and Genevieve Dailey. Thanks to Meriah Jacobs-Frost, Rob Frost, Lacee Mills, Chase Hirt, Molly Wilson, Melissa Atkins, Angie Haas, and Kristy McCann who provided assistance with photographs and graphics for the book. Special thanks to Jerry Jacobs for his countless hours of help with the calendar and photographs. Over the years, we have learned and acquired ideas from presenters at the South Dakota Kindergarten Academy, as well as from friends and colleagues, including Kim Hughes, Paulette Stefanik, Bonnie Walmsley, Deb Hoffmann, Abby Weber, Robert Whiteman, Pat Clark, Donna Williams, Gayle Bortnem, Bob Anderson, Tammy Weisser, Liz Venenga, Jean Hansen, Sarah Skatvold, Tammy Rusher, Roberta Gray, Becky Thomas, Lisa Carroll, Bridget Jacobs, and many others who generously shared their expertise and ideas. Thanks to Dean Lindstrom, Kevin Nelson, and their staff for their help in organizing the annual Kindergarten Academy for the teachers of the state. We would like to express our gratefulness to our acquisitions editor, Jessica Allan, as well as Joanna Coelho, editorial assistant, Amy Schroller, production editor, Peggie Howard, media editor, and Tomara Kafka, copy editor. To all who helped turn the dream of this book into a reality we express our gratitude.

The curriculum focal points used in the book are reprinted with permission from *Curriculum Focal Points for Prekindergarten through Grade 8 Mathematics: A Quest for Coherence*, copyright 2006 by the National Council of Teachers of Mathematics. All rights reserved. The *Curriculum Focal Points* identify key mathematical ideas for these grades. They are not discrete topics or a checklist to be mastered; rather, they provide a framework for the majority of instruction at a particular grade level and the foundation for future mathematics study. The complete document may be viewed at www.nctm.org/focalpoints.

About the Authors

 **Gera Jacobs** is a professor of early childhood education and taught kindergarten, preschool, and the elementary grades for many years. She has published articles in a number of national and regional journals and produced a CD ROM on inclusion for young children with special needs. She has presented at numerous state, regional, and national conferences, and has conducted many inservice presentations for teachers. She is a member of the National Association for the Education of Young Children (NAEYC) Governing Board and served on the NAEYC Affiliate Council. The Carnegie Corporation named her the South Dakota Professor of the Year in 2002. She was chairperson of the South Dakota Early Learning Guidelines Panel, responsible for writing the preschool standards for South Dakota.

Kathy Crowley is a kindergarten teacher and has taught kindergarten, preschool, and the elementary grades for many years. She was director of an after-school program and a member of the South Dakota Early Learning Guidelines Panel. Serving as a teacher-leader for a statewide mathematics initiative, she provides training to other teachers on innovative math strategies. An active member of several professional organizations, she has presented at numerous state, regional, and national conferences. Kathy served as vice-president of the South Dakota Association for the Education of Young Children and received the SDAEYC state service award in 2006. Her community named her the Teacher of the Year in 2007.

Gera and Kathy have helped to organize an annual statewide kindergarten academy for many years in South Dakota and have presented at kindergarten institutes in other states. They are the co-authors of *Play, Projects, and Preschool Standards: Nurturing Children's Sense of Wonder and Joy in Learning*, published by Corwin and winner of the 2008 Teachers' Choice Award, sponsored by *Learning Magazine* and the 2007 Distinguished Achievement Award from the Association of Educational Publishers. Gera and Kathy's collaboration began many years ago as team-teachers in a kindergarten classroom.

1

The Importance of the Kindergarten Year

Getting Off to a Good Start

All I Ever Really Needed to Know I Learned in Kindergarten

—Robert Fulghum

Most of what I really need to know about how to live, and what to do, and how to be, I learned in kindergarten . . . These are the things I learned: Share everything. Play fair. Don't hit people. Put things back where you found them. Clean up your own mess. Don't take things that aren't yours. Say you're sorry when you hurt somebody. Wash your hands before you eat. Flush. Warm cookies and cold milk are good for you. Live a balanced life. Learn some and think some and draw and paint and sing and dance and play and work some every day. . . . When you go out into the world, watch for traffic, hold hands, and stick together. Wonder (Fulghum, 1988, p. 2).

Kindergarten is a landmark year in the lives of children and their families. It is the first year of formal schooling for many children. Although many children attend preschool, kindergarten is often seen as the beginning of the elementary school years and can set the tone for children's educational future. Children at this age are excited about learning. They want to be part of the *community of learners* who can read and write as they see family and friends doing. We can build on that excitement to help children learn and meet standards in joy-filled, developmentally appropriate ways.

Children won't learn *everything* they'll ever need to know in kindergarten, but it is a place where we can help them build the foundation for much of what they will need in the future. Recent research indicates that the first five years of life are incredibly important to the development of children's brains. As children take part in activities in kindergarten, the nerve cells (neurons) in their brains are making connections that can last throughout their lifetimes and form the foundations for new connections. Playing with blocks, sand, water, and a variety of hands-on materials will help these connections (also called *synapses*) to form. As children listen to stories and express themselves through art and writing, more of these connections take shape. It is important that children have quality experiences in their first five years and beyond that promote this synaptic growth. With rich environments and opportunities for play and learning, children will have about 1,000 trillion synapses by the time they finish their kindergarten year (Gullo, 2006). This makes kindergarten an even more critical year in the life of a child, and one filled with potential to help children develop solid foundations for future learning.

As children begin to acquire new skills and knowledge their self-confidence will also blossom. This can begin a beautiful cycle of learning where children gain new understandings and build their sense of self-worth, which motivates them to learn even more and feel even better about themselves as the cycle continues. A developmentally appropriate kindergarten, where children are learning at their own levels in ways that are appropriate for their age through play, exploration, and engaging activities, will help children think of themselves as learners and ignite a flame inside that creates a desire to continue to discover and learn.

Developmentally Appropriate Practices

The National Association for the Education of Young Children's (NAEYC) document *Developmentally Appropriate Practices for Programs Serving Children Ages Birth through Age Eight* outlines best practices for implementing a quality kindergarten program. "Developmentally appropriate practice requires both meeting children where they are—which means that teachers must get to know them well—and enabling them to reach goals that are both challenging and achievable" (Copple & Bredekamp, 2009, p. xii). It is our role to continually make decisions about how best to meet our children's needs and intentionally plan experiences that will help them learn. As we do so, there are three key sources of knowledge we need to attend to (1) knowledge of how children develop and learn, (2) knowledge of each individual child in our program, and (3) knowledge of the social and cultural context of each of our children. This means we must know our children, respect them as members of their family and culture, and design experiences that are meaningful for them as individuals and will help them make progress in their development and learning (Copple & Bredekamp, 2009).

REACHING STANDARDS IN KINDERGARTEN AND THE POWER OF PLAY

There has been increased emphasis on standards and accountability throughout the educational system. This has had a profound impact on many kindergarten programs. Some teachers and administrators wonder how they can meet all the state and national standards that they are expected to achieve. With knowledge of the standards that children are expected to meet and knowledge about individual children in the classroom, kindergarten teachers can intentionally plan experiences that will help them learn in each of the content areas. Lilian Katz (2007) suggests not only focusing on content standards, but on the *standards of experience* that benefit each child:

- "Be intellectually engaged and absorbed.
- Be intellectually challenged.
- Be engaged in extended interactions.
- Be involved in sustained investigations of aspects of their own environment and experiences worthy of their interest, knowledge and understanding.
- Take the initiative in a range of activities and accept responsibility for what is accomplished.
- Experience the satisfaction that results from overcoming obstacles and setbacks and solving problems.
- Have confidence in their intellectual powers and questions.
- Help others to discover things and to understand them better.
- Make suggestions to others and express appreciation of others' efforts for what is accomplished.
- Apply their developing literacy and numeracy skills in purposeful ways.
- Feel that they belong to a group of their peers" (p. 95).

As we help our children meet content standards, we can ensure that they are getting the *standards of experience* that will enrich them as well.

Research has shown that play is one of the best ways for children of kindergarten age to learn. Through play, children are able to learn at their own pace. Play is motivating and maintains children's interest, enabling them to learn new skills. As children interact with engaging, hands-on materials they can be learning in all subject areas. There is no better way for children to learn geometry than by playing in the block area with a caring teacher who can help them experience shapes and their properties firsthand. Scientific understanding blossoms as young learners predict and observe objects sinking and floating in the water table. "Simply put, children talk more, integrate new knowledge, and are most engrossed and enthusiastic about learning while engaged in richly layered play" (Heidemann & Hewitt, 2010, p. 11).

What Research and the Experts Tell Us

Play and the History of Kindergarten

Frederick Froebel established the first kindergarten in 1837 in Germany. Froebel, who is credited with being the "father of kindergarten," believed that children learn best through play in a natural, informal environment. In his book, *The Education of Man,* Froebel (1887) wrote, "The mind grows by self revelation. In play the child ascertains what he can do, discovers his possibilities of will and thought by exerting his power spontaneously . . . In play he reveals his own original power" (p. vi). Froebel believed that children need free activity and opportunities to be creative. He understood that we need to nurture children's ability to play and created sets of blocks and other hands-on materials which he called *gifts* and *occupations.* He believed in active learning, including songs, stories,

(Continued)

(Continued)

games, and opportunities to learn from interacting socially with others. Using Froebel's theories, Susan Elizabeth Blow instituted the first public kindergarten in the United States in 1873 in St. Louis. Like Froebel, Blow recognized the importance of having well-educated teachers who understand how children learn best. Both of them devoted a great deal of their time to training teachers, as well as working with the children. Over the years, researchers have continued to affirm the importance of play as one of the best ways for kindergarten children to learn and meet standards. Many of our top educational theorists have emphasized the power of play for children's learning, including Piaget, Dewey, Brunner, and Vygotsky who called play "the preeminent educational activity" for our children (Berk & Winsler, 1995, p. 57).

There are many developmentally appropriate experiences teachers can plan for children that will help them meet standards. Children benefit from both large and small group experiences, as well as time to work individually. They gain from both child-guided and adult-guided experiences (Epstein, 2007). Knowing children's interests can help teachers plan long-term studies that capture and sustain children's attention. Children can learn in all areas of the curriculum as they read about, research, and learn more about the topics they are studying. There is great potential for children to cultivate new skills as they begin to represent what they are learning through drawing, writing, speaking, painting, sculpting, and other forms of expression. Learning about subject areas in the context of a long-term study or investigation can make learning more meaningful and, therefore, help children better remember and use what they have learned.

READY FOR THE CHILDREN

Nationally, there is increased awareness of the importance of the kindergarten year. When the president and 50 governors convened to form the National Educational Goals Panel in 1990 to improve teaching and learning for the country's children, the first goal they established was that *All children will start school ready to learn*. This sparked a nationwide effort to ensure that children received the health care, nutrition, physical activity, and education experiences they needed to get off to a good start in school. Children are naturally ready to learn; however, there is a great deal that needs to be done in order to help children be more *successful* in kindergarten and future school years. This includes making sure children have their basic needs met and that their families have sufficient resources to support them. Part of the ready-to-learn goal is that every parent will be their child's first teacher, spend time each day helping their children learn, and receive the training and support they need in order to be able to do this (National Governors Association, 2005).

Instead of looking at readiness as something solely within children, we need to have ready schools and ready communities to support our children in order for them to be successful in kindergarten. It is our job as kindergarten teachers to welcome each child who comes through our doors and be ready ourselves to help make this year the best beginning possible.

TRANSITION TO KINDERGARTEN AND FORMING PARTNERSHIPS WITH FAMILIES

One way to ensure that children will be as successful as possible is to plan their transition into kindergarten. A smooth transition can make a tremendous difference, not only in kindergarten but in their attitude toward schooling as they proceed through the grades (Pianta & Kraft-Sayer, 2003). Simple planning and activities can make a large impact. However, to have a lasting influence, transitions need to involve families, begin before the school year starts, and continue throughout the first several weeks or even months of school. Many parents find that they feel comfortable with the routines of their children's preschool and child care settings. With the changes kindergarten brings, parents will also benefit from a thoughtfully planned transition, which helps them feel welcomed and begins productive, back and forth communication. There are many types of transition activities you can plan, depending on your circumstances and the children you teach.

Making home visits is a wonderful way to begin to form relationships with children and families and learn more about them. Asking about children's interests, favorite books, songs, strengths, and needs can help with planning a curriculum that corresponds with children's current skill levels, gains their attention, and motivates them right from the start. A home visit can provide the opportunity to learn more about children's cultural backgrounds as well. Visits are helpful for children who are shy or have a hard time warming up to new situations and people, resulting in less trauma and tears the first week of school. They also assist us in understanding children who might otherwise demonstrate challenging behaviors, which may be prevented if we know more about their interests, motivations, and concerns. The more we understand children's social and cultural contexts, the more developmentally appropriate kindergarten we will be able to offer for all of our children.

If home visits aren't feasible, invite parents, guardians, and children in for short, scheduled visits at the beginning of the year. Mail letters or postcards that welcome families to the new school year, sharing your excitement and some events for the year ahead. This message or an e-mail could also invite them to drop by the week before school starts while you are working on setting up the classroom, including one evening to accommodate families' schedules. Realizing the importance of the transition to kindergarten, some schools arrange these visits during the first few days of school instead of having all of the children start on the opening day. In these schools, small groups of four or five children and their parents and guardians spend part of the day during the first week. The following week the entire class begins together.

Transition activities can begin the spring before kindergarten and include meetings with preschool teachers to share information. Many schools plan *kindergarten round-up* events as a way to bring children and families into the school, begin the registration process, and learn more about the kindergarten program. This is an excellent opportunity to begin a reciprocal relationship with families. Evening events can be planned for parents and guardians to provide information about the school and curriculum, show them around the room, share schedules, and help them fill out necessary forms. The following day children can be invited to spend an hour or so in the kindergarten classroom to take part in a few fun activities. Some schools like to have children join the current kindergarten class for these events, while others choose to have the children in smaller, more intimate groups. If the community doesn't have a comprehensive program for screening three- and four-year-old children to identify special needs, children can also take part in a nonthreatening screening, including vision and hearing, to know how to better meet children's needs when they arrive. Round-up events can be a good start to the kindergarten transition, allowing children and families to meet teachers, administrators, and future classmates. They can also help families feel welcomed and secure from the beginning.

Try This!

At round-up or during opening transition activities with families, give them a monthly calendar with activities they can do with their children each day, such as *Count the doors and windows in your home.* The activities should be simple and require little preparation time for the parents. The Resources section of this book contains monthly calendars that could be sent home, beginning with August of the kindergarten year and extending through the summer leading up to first grade. The suggestions provide ideas that families can use to help their children meet kindergarten standards, reinforcing what is learned at school. The calendars can be personalized by adding upcoming field trip dates, events, or opportunities for families to volunteer and get involved, specific to your program. It may be most effective to send the calendar home each month with a suggestion that families hang it on their refrigerators and replace it when a new one comes home the following month. Some communities give out free magnets with emergency contact information that they would be happy to share with teachers to send home with the calendars.

If funds are available, provide each family with a paperback book to read together, encouraging them to read to their children each day. A book such as *Mamma Loves You* by Caroline Stutson is a good choice for this purpose; it's easy to read, predictable, and shares a message about the love parents have for children. Instead of purchasing books for each family, you could also have books to lend from your classroom or school library. Children can take a different book home when they have returned the one they currently have.

Some teachers enjoy hosting family picnics, potlucks, or other play events before the start of the school year. This is a good way to meet the children and families, as well as for families to get to know one another. Parent-teacher organizations, United Way, or other community groups may be willing to help fund transition efforts to help this important year get off to a good start. Once the school year begins, hold an open house at a convenient time for families to further introduce them to the activities their children are doing.

Try This!

Setting up centers or interest areas for parents or guardians to visit with their kindergartener is a wonderful way to introduce them to the classroom. These centers may include a math area where they make simple patterns with colored blocks, a science/discovery area where families plant flowers or bean seeds together, and an art area where they draw pictures of their families. There could also be a simple snack area where families prepare and eat snacks together. This might include measuring out ingredients for a simple snack mix with written directions for them to follow.

STRENGTHENING RELATIONSHIPS

Creating meaningful relationships with families extends and strengthens children's learning. Research has shown that the more parents are involved in their children's education the better outcomes their children will have (Arndt & McGuire-Schwartz, 2008; Knopf & Swick, 2008). There are many ways to involve families throughout the year. Invite parents, guardians, and grandparents to volunteer in the classroom to read to children, help them with skills such as learning to tie shoes, or write stories on the computer.

What Research and the Experts Tell Us

When the National Governors Association's Task Force on School Readiness wrote their final report in 2005, they emphasized the need to focus on classroom quality. Research has shown that the quality of our classrooms and teaching and the interactions between teachers and children are critical to student learning. The Classroom Assessment Scoring System (CLASS) developed by the Center for Advanced Study of Teaching and Learning was designed to measure the quality of these interactions. CLASS describes three domains of classroom quality that need to be considered. The first domain, **Emotional Support**, includes the dimensions of *Positive Climate, Teacher Sensitivity,* and *Regard for Student Perspective.* The second domain, **Classroom Organization,** includes *Behavior Management, Productivity,* and *Instructional Learning Formats.* The final dimension, **Instructional Support**, consists of *Concept Development, Quality Feedback,* and *Language Modeling.* Research has shown that when teachers excel in these dimensions, their students also excel, learn more, and have higher outcomes. Information about CLASS can be found at http://www.classobservation.com/ (Pianta, LaParo, & Hamre, 2008).

MEETING THE NEEDS OF ALL CHILDREN

It is critical that kindergartens meet the needs of all of our children. The final report of the National Governors Association Task Force on School Readiness (2005) described *Ready Schools* as those that demonstrate a commitment to the success of every child, regardless of his or her prior experiences, family and economic circumstances, linguistic and cultural background, and natural abilities and interests. These schools adopt curriculum and instruction methods that are research-based and support high standards. . . . Moreover, they are responsive to individual children's needs, provide environments that are conducive to learning and exploration, and incorporate children with special needs in regular classrooms whenever possible. Ready schools also ensure that second-language learners receive age-appropriate, culturally sensitive, and challenging curriculum instruction (p. 21).

Throughout this book there will be suggestions for helping the many diverse learners in our classrooms, including English Language Learners, children with special needs, as well as those who are gifted.

SUPPORTING CHILDREN LEARNING ENGLISH AS A NEW LANGUAGE

Children who are learning English as a new language and their families will need additional consideration as they make the transition to kindergarten. Interpreters who can translate when we meet with families are essential. Providing written material in the language of each of the families is also important. There are software programs and Web sites available that translate written materials, including http://wordmonkey.info or http://babelfish.yahoo.com. It is a good idea to ask someone who speaks the language to look over any translated materials to ensure that the meaning has been translated clearly. Keep in mind that when writing anything that will be translated, use simple, clear language without idiomatic expressions that might be difficult to understand in another language, such as "hang in there." Let families know you honor and value their culture and language and invite them to share some of their language and traditions with the children throughout the year.

WORKING WITH CHILDREN'S INDIVIDUAL NEEDS

Planning the transition to kindergarten is especially critical for children with special needs. Ideally, this begins a year ahead of the transition by forming a team that includes the family, preschool and kindergarten teachers, therapists, and administrators. The first step is to find out as much as possible about the child, including strengths and needs. Designing a strong Individual Education Plan (IEP) with the team that outlines goals for the child and how the goals can best be met will be a key component. The plan should include the transition and how it can best be accomplished. This will involve cooperation and planning by all involved.

With the wide range of ages, as well as socioeconomic and cultural backgrounds found in many kindergartens today, there is an expansive array of skills and abilities children bring with them to the kindergarten setting. Meeting all of their needs is challenging. Knowing children's strengths and needs, including those who have special needs as well as those who are more advanced, will help us to make sure they are receiving the support they need. Talking with families and keeping communication flowing throughout the year will help to ensure that all children are continuing to progress and learn.

Summary

Kindergarten is an important milestone in the educational lives of children. A positive kindergarten experience makes it much more likely that the coming years of schooling will also be positive. Research has demonstrated that the first five years are especially important to children's future brain development. Kindergarten provides a tremendous opportunity to help children build a strong foundation in all areas of development. This can be done best by providing a wealth of hands-on activities where children can learn through play and exploration, with the guidance of a caring teacher who intentionally plans experiences for them. Research has shown that play is one of the best ways for children in kindergarten to learn and has been an integral part of kindergarten since it was established. Forming relationships with families and ongoing communication with them is critical. Helping children make a smooth transition to kindergarten makes it more likely that the year will be successful for both children and their families. Our role is to welcome children, with their many unique gifts and needs, and provide them with a strong, developmentally appropriate kindergarten that will not only help them reach standards, but provide them with experiences that will ignite a love of learning that can last a lifetime.

2

Designing the Kindergarten Environment

Designing an engaging environment that promotes wonder, a sense of community, and real joy in learning is one of our first and most important roles. Children will learn more in a setting that encourages them to explore, is sensitive to their needs and interests, and invites them to new learning every day.

CREATING A WELCOMING ENVIRONMENT

Our goal is to create an environment that welcomes children and their families the moment they walk through the door. Having children's names displayed around the room helps children and families see that this is a place where they belong. Children's names can appear on a welcoming bulletin board and used to label personal spaces, such as coat hooks and cubbies where students keep their individual supplies. Prominently displaying children's work on walls and bulletin boards also assures them that this is their place.

Try This!

Designate a bulletin board or wall space as a classroom art museum that has a homemade frame allocated for each child's work with the child's name prominently written under it. Consider making homemade frames as kindergarten teacher Faith Tieszen does from construction paper, folding the edges and corners of the paper up to add dimension. Each child can be involved in choosing which piece of art to display in the frame and in changing it throughout the year to keep it fresh and appealing.

Invite parents and guardians to bring in photographs of their families to display in clear plastic acrylic frames. Children could take turns bringing home a disposable camera to take pictures of family and pets.

Family photos can be placed at children's eye level where they can easily access them. Children should feel free to bring their family photos to the area where they are playing or resting.

There is no need to have the room completely decorated when the children walk in the door on the first day. It helps children feel more connected to the room if they are able to have some part in setting up and decorating it. Each child could place his or her family photo in a special spot in the room and create a piece of art to hang. Letting your children know that you would like to add their artwork to the classroom art museum will give them a reason to do their very best and feel a sense of pride when they see it displayed.

Making sure the room reflects the culture of each of our children also helps to create a welcoming atmosphere. It is important that each of our children see themselves reflected in the books, dolls, and other materials around the room to help nurture their sense of belonging. Parents can be good resources for providing suggestions and materials from their cultures and can be invited to come in and share their customs. Multicultural items, from a wide variety of cultures, may also broaden children's understanding and appreciation for others. Including posters, instruments, and music from other cultures may also help children develop respect for these cultures. Adding multicultural fabrics around the room or at the windows adds interest, absorbs sound, and adds to the home-like, peaceful feel of the room.

At the beginning of the school year when some children may still be hesitant to join in, it can be helpful to have familiar items around the room that may provide them with a source of comfort. This could include a housekeeping area with common household items or a play dough area with cookie cutters and other everyday objects to use in their play. Placing a welcoming table near the entrance to the classroom can help reluctant children gradually ease into the routine of the day. This table might include art materials, simple puzzles, or table toys that children can play with independently or where they can simply observe their peers at play (Hyson, 2004).

Add items to the room throughout the year to spark children's curiosity, such as prisms, hanging crystals, or other light catchers. Beaded curtains can help divide areas, as well as add to the décor of the room (Curtis & Carter, 2003). Trips to unique stores can become treasure hunts as you search for items to add a little sparkle and wonder to your classroom.

Organize the room so that materials are clearly labeled and accessible to students. Including both words and pictures on the labels helps our emerging readers begin to associate the words with the objects. It also helps them to return items where they belong and develop their sense of responsibility.

Each day, engage the children in choosing an object in the room to label. Some teachers like to put each child's name on a craft stick, stored in a decorated can or mug. Each day, they pull out one child's name to choose an object to label. The child's stick will then go into another container until everyone has had a turn. Invite the designated child to select an object to label. Using index cards or brightly colored paper write out the name of the item with the children, sounding out each letter as you write it. Ask the child to tape the label to the object so it can be read throughout the year. Labeling one item each day allows children to focus on one particular word and how it is formed. Taking part in the making of the label makes the words more meaningful and helps children start learning letter-sound connections. These labels also support children's writing throughout the year.

Consider adding a second label with the word in another language, such as Spanish or another language spoken by a child in the room. This could be done with every label or only those words that would be especially useful in learning the new language. A simple picture dictionary, such as *The Usborne First Thousand Words in Spanish*, is very helpful for this task. Web sites, such as http://www.google.com/ig or http://babelfish.yahoo.com can also provide a quick translation in a variety of languages. Designate a specific color for each language, such as blue for English or red for Spanish.

Try This!

To make labeling objects in the room more motivating, provide a fun name for the job, such as the *Label Lemur*. Change the title of this honor throughout the year as another way to increase vocabulary. The Label Lemur could be called the *Lemur de la Etiqueta* when labeling objects in Spanish. A sample Label Lemur name badge can be found in the Resource section of this book. The name badge could be attached to cardstock and laminated for more durability.

KINDERGARTEN ROOM DESIGN

Meeting Area

The meeting area in the kindergarten room is an important place where children gather in large and small groups, listen to stories, and begin to form a classroom community. A large colorful rug can help define the area, as well as add a layer of comfort; carpet squares serve a similar purpose. It is helpful to position this area near a chalk board or whiteboard and near a blank wall or bulletin board where you can create a word wall. At the beginning of the year, the word wall can start out with each of the children's names, with new words added throughout the year as children learn new sight words and words related to the topics they are investigating.

It is helpful to have an easel in this area to hold big books or other charts to share with the children. Having a basket of supplies that can be used during group time is also very helpful. This can include markers, chalk, pencils, scrap paper, supplies for calendar activities, pointers, and anything else needed for work in this area.

Try This!

Book Benches

To increase your storage space and help children to see better during group activities, try making book benches. Start with sturdy plastic crates. To make the seat, cut a piece of plywood two inches longer and wider than the top of the crate. Many home supply stores will cut the plywood.

Cover the board with heavy canvas fabric which can be fixed in place under the board with a staple gun. Drill two holes toward the back of the plywood seat. Add foam padding before attaching the fabric to create a more cushioned seat if desired. Insert heavy-duty plastic cable ties into the holes and use as hinges to fasten the board to the crate, creating a lid that can be opened. The book benches are a good place to store books and can keep them sorted by genre, season, topic, or author. Kindergarten teacher Jean Hansen constructed these benches for her classroom to create a multilevel seating arrangement, with some children sitting on the floor, while others could sit behind them on the benches. The benches helped to decrease the dreaded *"I can't see the book!"* comment that may come from having all the children sitting on one level. They can also serve as small tables for children sitting on the floor or clustered together to form a larger table.

DESIGNING INTEREST AREAS THAT INVITE LEARNING

Research confirms that one of the most effective developmentally appropriate ways for kindergarten children to learn is through hands-on interactions with engaging materials and the support of a caring adult. This can happen by setting up areas around the room with rich interesting materials where children can have these experiences. These *interest areas* might include library/reading, writing, math, science/discovery, sand and water, computer, and dramatic play (Dodge, Colker, & Heroman, 2002). Other areas can be added depending on children's interests and materials available. Interest areas can be the hub of engaging learning in the kindergarten classroom by allowing children to be actively involved in exploring and providing a place where they can practice the many skills they have been learning. Interest areas are ideal places for children to learn kindergarten standards and encompass all of the subjects included in the standards. Simply being able to see the math manipulatives in the math area, science materials in the science/discovery area, and writing tools in the writing area helps children learn how to categorize, sort, and gain other skills important to learning math and literacy standards.

Interest areas can be created in any available space by thinking creatively about how to most effectively use tables, walls, corners, and floor space. Many teachers choose not to use their tables as assigned seating for children in order to be able to use them in interest areas. Instead, children have labeled cubbies where they can keep all their materials and a coat hook for jackets and book bags.

When possible, it is wise to separate quiet areas from noisy ones. File cabinets or moveable shelving can help divide one area from another.

Adding magnetic letters or numbers to the file cabinet transforms it into a learning center itself. Adding pencils, paper, and other writing materials adds literacy to any area of the room.

Library/Reading Area

A quality library/reading area can be the heart of a literacy-rich, kindergarten classroom. Displaying books with their front covers visible invites children to pick them up and experience the joy of interacting with a special book. This can be done with a book display rack which can be purchased or made. Books can also be displayed on shelves, chalkboard ledges, or on plastic gutters attached to the wall. To make the area more cozy, add floor pillows, bean bag chairs, or other soft features.

Materials for the Library/Reading Area

- ☐ Display rack
- ☐ Children's picture books, both fiction and nonfiction
- ☐ Children's magazines
- ☐ Books made by children in the classroom
- ☐ Floor pillows or bean bag chairs

Listening Area

A listening area allows children to hear books read, even when there are no adults available to read to them. Books on tape or CD can be made with your children, purchased, or borrowed from a library.

Materials for the Listening Area

- ☐ Tape recorder or CD player with headphones
- ☐ Adaptors for multiple headsets
- ☐ Recloseable bags with individual books

Writing Area

A writing area encourages children to engage in additional literacy activities throughout the day. Provide organized storage that can hold a variety of paper, pencils, markers, and other writing materials. As the year progresses, add notebooks, homemade blank books, and other items to encourage children to write.

Materials for the Writing Area

- ☐ Variety of paper
- ☐ Notebooks
- ☐ Pencils, crayons, washable markers
- ☐ Chalkboards, whiteboards
- ☐ Alphabet
- ☐ Rubber stamps with washable ink pads

Computer Area

Providing a computer with quality software for children to use can promote children's writing and learning in all areas of the curriculum. Consider setting up a Web page with picture cues of quality, appropriate Web sites with hyperlinks the children can click on to independently open the sites.

Materials for the Computer Area

- ☐ Computer
- ☐ Two seats to promote cooperative learning
- ☐ Quality software and Internet sites

Science/Discovery Area

An appealing science/discovery area attracts children's attention and draws them into exploration and inquiry. There are advantages to locating this area near a window if possible where growing plants can receive needed light. Children can look out the window to check weather conditions and observe clouds and other natural features outside. Provide engaging materials that encourage investigation and change them throughout the year to retain children's eagerness in discovering more about their world.

Materials for the Science/Discovery Area

- ☐ Magnifying glasses and tripod magnifier
- ☐ Natural materials, such as rocks, shells, pinecones, and leaves
- ☐ Small aquarium or fish bowl or other classroom pet
- ☐ Living plants
- ☐ Magnets and a variety of materials to use with them
- ☐ Pulleys, gears, wheels, and inclined planes
- ☐ Balance scale

Math Area

The math area is a place where children can be learning math standards as they have fun playing with a variety of manipulatives.

Materials for the Math Area

- ☐ Number line
- ☐ Variety of math manipulatives, such as Unifix® cubes and jumbo Cuisenaire Rods®
- ☐ Multicultural and natural materials for counting and sorting, such as shells and large beads

- ☐ Small colored blocks, keys, buttons, milk lids, or other common materials for counting, sorting, and making patterns
- ☐ Paper, pencils, clipboards, and graph paper
- ☐ Rulers, meter sticks, and other materials for measuring
- ☐ Calculators with large numbers
- ☐ Abacus
- ☐ Counting books and other math-related picture books

Block Area

The block area helps children learn skills that support them in meeting standards in many domains, including social and emotional, motor, and language. The block area becomes a natural extension of our math area with children learning geometry concepts as they play with a variety of shapes and sizes and join blocks together to form different shapes. Large numbers of blocks allow for more developed constructions. Add to your block set over time as your budget allows.

Materials for the Block Area

- ☐ Wooden unit blocks of assorted shapes and sizes
- ☐ Large hollow blocks, cardboard bricks, or other large building blocks
- ☐ Materials to extend children's play in the area, which could include
  - ○ Rainbow blocks with colored acrylic plastic windows
  - ○ Block people representing diverse cultures
  - ○ Toy animals and transportation toys, such as cars and trucks

Try This!

Putting wooden blocks away can become more of a learning activity and a little less of a burden by trying this idea. Line the block shelves with bulletin board paper or paper made especially for lining shelves. Trace the outline of each type of wooden block to show where it fits on the shelf.

If you have a large number of blocks and have had trouble getting them all put away, start the block area cleanup a couple of minutes before the general clean up. Ask each child playing in the area to choose a shape or two that they will be responsible for putting away. Involve other children who are willing to help by giving them each a specific shape of block. Children learn sorting and classifying skills necessary for success in mathematics as they put the blocks away. If you don't have to share the room with another group and have enough room, consider allowing children to keep their constructions up for a few days, or even longer, to allow them to make more elaborate, complex structures, and eliminating the stress this daily task sometimes causes.

Art Area

An art area with a variety of art materials is an excellent place for children to develop their creativity and imagination. It is helpful to locate this area near a sink, if one is available, and away from the doorway so paint spills are less of a problem.

Materials for the Art Area

- ❐ Art easel(s) with room for two or more children
- ❐ Variety of paper, paint, and brushes
- ❐ Crayons, washable markers
- ❐ Glue, paste, tape, and scissors
- ❐ Play dough, clay, and other modeling materials
- ❐ Multicultural paint, crayons, paper, and markers
- ❐ Additional materials to spark interest and imagination, varied over time, such as craft sticks, small pom-poms, pipe cleaners, glitter, wood scraps, and fabric

Dramatic Play Area

An inviting dramatic play area can begin as a housekeeping area and later transform to complement the topics you are investigating with the children. Adding writing materials, including paper, notepads, and pencils encourages children to make lists or cards. Include multicultural dolls, fabrics, and clothing.

Materials for the Dramatic Play Area

- ❐ Table and chairs
- ❐ Play refrigerator, sink, and stove
- ❐ Plastic cookware and dishware
- ❐ Multicultural baby dolls with clothes and doll bed
- ❐ Clocks and calendar
- ❐ Posters

❏ Dress-up clothes

❏ Additional items to convert the area to match topics of study throughout the year

Sand and Water Area

A sand table and water table are great additions to the kindergarten classroom. Children can be learning math, science, language, and social skills as they play in sand and water. Many children also find these materials very soothing. These are excellent materials to have outside when weather allows. If you do not have a sand or water table, you can make your own by simply using large dishwashing tubs.

Materials for the Sand and Water Area

❏ Sand table or plastic container for sand

❏ Water table or plastic container for water

❏ Measuring cups and a variety of small containers

❏ Plastic tubing

❏ Water and sand wheels

❏ Sifters

Additional Areas and Centers

Some teachers like to have a music area, woodworking area, puzzles and table toys, as well as a puppet theater available every day, while others set these up less frequently to provide new activities to spark curiosity. It is a good idea to change or add to the materials in each of the interest areas throughout the year to keep children's interest at a high level. Some teachers use the word *center* interchangeably with *interest area*. Centers could also be thought of as more temporary or individual activities set up within an interest area. Individual center activities can be placed in a variety of motivating containers, including baskets, spare backpacks, or colorful plastic containers. There are many benefits to having interest areas in the kindergarten classroom. Interest areas or centers:

- Provide children with the opportunity to learn and practice skills in all areas of the standards
- Offer opportunities for children to develop and use language
- Give teachers the chance to work with individuals and small groups while others are happily playing and learning
- Help children develop positive approaches to learning, including persistence, initiative, curiosity, eagerness, problem solving, and imagination
- Give children freedom of movement so needed at their age
- Provide children with the opportunity to make choices and develop responsibility
- Contribute to children's social and emotional development
- Offer opportunities for children to be creative and experience the joy of learning

Try This!

Let visitors to your room better understand all the standards children are reaching as they work in interest areas by putting signs in each of the areas. The signs can simply contain the name of the area and a list of standard areas children will be introduced to in that area, such as

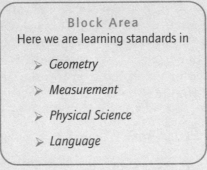

Block Area
Here we are learning standards in

➤ *Geometry*

➤ *Measurement*

➤ *Physical Science*

➤ *Language*

The signs could also contain more specific benchmarks from national or state standards.

MANAGING INTEREST AREAS

Introduce children to the interest areas and materials at the beginning of the year. Clarify your expectations for them while they are at the interest areas. These expectations could include

- Treat classmates and materials with respect
- Return all materials where they belong
- Walk from one area to another

Ideally, there should be a variety of activities and materials children can choose from in the interest areas. In their book, *Developmentally Appropriate Practices in Early Childhood Programs,* the National Association for the Education of Young Children (NAEYC) recommends that kindergarten children have "extended periods of time in learning centers (60 minutes or more in full-day and at least 45 minutes in half-day kindergarten) so that children are able to get deeply involved in an activity at a complex level . . . Children have ample time and opportunity to investigate what sparks their curiosity" (Copple & Bredekamp, 2009, p. 222).

There are many ways to manage your interest-area time to make it productive learning time, as well as an opportunity for creativity and play. In a full-day kindergarten program, one might designate the morning interest-area time as a time where children can choose activities at the library/reading, listening, writing, science, math, computer, and art areas. There may be other special activities that go along with the current topic of study. Then in the afternoon, children choose from these areas, as well as all the other areas, including blocks, sand and water, and dramatic play. In a half-day program, interest-area time might be divided in a similar fashion, with the second part allowing for more choices. Each week, choose specific activities in some or all of the areas that you would like each child to complete or materials you would like for them to work with during interest-area time. Place a sign-up sheet next to those activities where children can either sign their name or check off their name when they have completed the activity. Another option is to make a weekly interest area log with pictures representing each area. Each child can check off an area once he or she has visited it that week. Ask children to participate in each area at least once before the end of the week. The log will help you monitor to ensure that all children have experiences that help them meet standards in all areas of the curriculum.

The number of chairs in an area, such as at a writing or art table, lets children know how many children can be there at one time. With practice and our support, children will become adept at figuring out whether an area is too crowded for them.

To make a smooth transition from group time to interest-area time, try naming each of the areas and asking who would like to start out in that area, dismissing children as they choose an area. This is another way to manage the number of students in each area. With guidance, most children will be able to choose an area where they want to begin and then continue to move from area to area on their own as their interests lead them.

Occasionally, there may be a new activity or material that all the children want to use for extended periods of time, such as a new piece of software or new props in the dramatic-play area. For these high-demand activities, it will be helpful to have a sign-up sheet for those interested. Several children can be appointed to the area each day and others will know that they will have time another day.

Some teachers like to make a choice board with a picture of each interest area on it and spaces denoting how many children comfortably fit in the area. Next to the board they have clothespins or magnetic clips with each child's name and sometimes the child's photograph attached. As children decide which area to go to, they put their clips on the picture of that area. When the spaces for a particular area are filled, children know they need to choose a different one. When children want to move onto another area, they move their clip to the corresponding area on the choice board. Other teachers use a pocket chart for their choice board. Each row has one interest area labeled with words, a picture, and the number of children the area can hold. Children put cards with their names in the row with the interest area of their choice.

The advantage to having children choose their area, activities, and amount of time in each area is that it gives them responsibility for making good learning choices and provides them with the opportunity to grow in their decision making. Providing children with choice is highly motivating, and they are more likely to learn when they are interested and motivated. Empowering children to choose their own materials will also help them develop initiative and independence. As children work with materials they have chosen, they will also develop self-confidence and see themselves as capable learners. This sense of self-worth can propel their desire to learn even more and develop positive approaches to learning.

THE SOCIAL ENVIRONMENT

A welcoming environment is not just the physical space but also the social atmosphere we help to create. Taking time to engage in conversations with children individually helps us get to know them better and can help them to know we value them. Designing the room so that children can easily work and play cooperatively with each other will also help to create the community of learners' atmosphere that allows each child to blossom.

Kindergarten children come to us from a variety of backgrounds and experiences. They are exposed to violence on television, in movies, and sometimes in their daily lives. All children need a secure, safe environment in order to thrive (Levin & Kilbourne, 2008). We can provide that stable, nurturing environment for at least the hours they are with us. Try to avoid rushing children; a calm, productive environment helps children learn more than hurrying them from one activity to the next. Provide places where children can work side by side with others, as well as places for them to get away when they feel a need to be by themselves, such as soft, cozy floor pillows where they can curl up with a good book in the library area. Playing soft music while children are working and playing in interest areas can add to a calm atmosphere. Warm daily greetings as children arrive let them know this is a place where they belong. At the end of the day, let them know of a fun activity you'll be doing together the next school day and assure them that you will look forward to seeing them.

SCHEDULING TO MAKE THE MOST OF OUR TIME TOGETHER

Getting off to a Positive Start

A positive start to the day can smooth the way for everything else that follows. Greeting children by name as they walk in the door can help them feel welcomed and may help to overcome negative experiences they may have encountered before they arrived. Offering a 10–15 minute welcoming time where children put away jackets, return notes and library books, and catch up on the latest news with their friends gives you time to greet each child and any family who may be there to drop off their children (Fisher, 1998).

Before children arrive set out books, puzzles, and other easy-to-clean-up materials for children to play with during this time. You could also designate a couple of areas children could use at this time, such as the library/reading area and table toys.

Signing In

During welcoming time, children can also sign in. At the beginning of the year, children can simply sign their first names on a sheet of paper. Once they have mastered this, they can move on to writing their first name and last initial, and then their first and last names.

Try This!

Customize your sign-in sheets to go along with the topics you are studying. You could have apple-shaped paper when studying apples, or paper decorated with rubber stamps or other pictures. Once a week or so have two or more sign-in sheets; let children know that when there are multiple sheets, their task is to sign in under their favorite symbol. For example, you might have one sheet with a picture of a red apple and the word *red,* one with *yellow,* and one with *green.* Children can sign in under their favorite color of apple. Adding slices of each type of apple will make this even more meaningful and enjoyable! Have the words *What do you like most?* on a strip of paper next to the sheets. Use the data on the sign-in sheets to make graphs with the children, showing the number who chose each option, and then talking about which was most, least, or the same.

A predictable, yet flexible, schedule makes it easier for children to know what to expect throughout the day. Think about each part of the day as potential for learning and building relationships. Snack time offers a wonderful opportunity for conversations between you and the children and time for children to converse with each other. Allow children's interests and needs to guide your planning and the timing when possible. Post your schedule with words and photographs of the children engaged in activities that illustrate that particular part of the schedule. The following schedules provide examples of the way the kindergarten day might be arranged.

Full-Day Kindergarten Schedule		
8:30–8:45	15 minutes	Welcoming time (greetings, hang up coats, unpack, sign-in, turn in notes from home, return library books, quiet designated activities)
8:45–9:00	15 minutes	Class meeting, opening activities, and calendar (lunch count, weather, calendar activities, count days in kindergarten, etc.)
9:00–9:20	20 minutes	Shared literacy (shared reading with poems, songs, charts, and big books)
9:20–9:45	25 minutes	Writers' workshop (shared writing, interactive writing, mini-lessons, individual writing time, individual writing conferences, author's chair)
9:45–10:00	15 minutes	Snack and conversation
10:00–10:20	20 minutes	Outside recess
10:20–11:30	70 minutes	Interest areas and work on special topics of study
11:30–11:45	15 minutes	Sharing and cleanup
11:45–12:45	60 minutes	Lunch and recess
12:45–1:15	30 minutes	Rest, independent reading, and read aloud
1:15–2:00	45 minutes	Math and science explorations (mini-lesson, study or project-related activity, math and/or science related centers)
2:00–3:10	70 minutes	Specials (physical education, music, library, guidance, art, etc.), outside recess, snack, choice time, and social studies investigations
3:10–3:30	20 minutes	Review of the day/planning for tomorrow closing story and song (children and teacher share and reflect on activities of the day, plan for tomorrow, read favorite stories, sing goodbye songs)

		Half-Day Kindergarten Schedule
8:20–8:30	10 minutes	Welcoming time (hang up coats, unpack, sign-in, turn in notes from home, return library books, quiet designated activities)
8:30–8:45	15 minutes	Class meeting, opening activities, and calendar (weather, calendar, patterns, count days in kindergarten, etc.)
8:45–9:05	20 minutes	Shared literacy (shared reading with poems, songs, charts, and big books)
9:05–9:25	20 minutes	Writers' workshop (shared writing, interactive writing, mini-lessons, individual writing time, individual writing conferences, author's chair)
9:25–10:25	60 minutes	Interest areas, work on special topics of study, and social studies investigations
10:25–10:40	15 minutes	Snack and conversation
10:40–10:55	15 minutes	Outside recess
10:55–11:20	25 minutes	Math and science explorations (mini-lesson, study or project-related activity, math and/or science related centers), and specials
11:20–11:30	10 minutes	Review of the day/planning for tomorrow, closing story and song (children and teacher share and reflect on activities of the day, plan for tomorrow, read favorite stories, sing goodbye songs)

SUPPORTING CHILDREN LEARNING ENGLISH AS A NEW LANGUAGE

A welcoming environment helps kindergarten children learning English as a new language to feel comfortable and more willing to try the new words they are learning. Labeling the names of objects around the room in their home languages, as well as English, helps both children and their families in their language acquisition. Engaging interest areas, where children are able to learn at their own pace, also gives you the opportunity to work with children individually. Expand children's language by pointing out the names of materials they are playing with and joining in their play, while modeling simple and clear language. Engage in conversations whenever possible to provide additional opportunities to use English.

WORKING WITH CHILDREN'S INDIVIDUAL NEEDS

It is important to set up the environment so that each child can participate as fully as possible. Make any needed accommodations to the floor plan or interest areas to meet children's needs. Tables, easels, water tables, and other equipment can be raised, lowered, or adapted to suit children's requirements. Make sure all areas are wheelchair accessible if necessary. Provide adaptive equipment for children who need it in order to participate as fully as possible. Pair up children with visual or motor challenges with classmates who can help them with equipment and materials. Three-minute hourglass timers can help children with attention issues increase their persistence and make an effort to stay at an area for at least a few minutes at a time. Including plenty of time in the schedule for children to work and play in interest areas gives you time to work individually with children who are having difficulty, as well as provide enriching activities for children who have already mastered concepts. Interest areas provide opportunities for children to work at their own individual level and progress as they are ready.

Summary

Designing a child-friendly environment with interest areas in each content area helps children meet standards and promotes learning in developmentally appropriate ways. Engaging materials and activities in the interest areas provide children the opportunity to practice the skills they have been learning. It is important to create a positive climate that is reflective and respectful of children's diversity. Periodically adding new, interesting materials that encourage exploration and wonder can keep children motivated. To ensure optimal use of these learning environments, a predictable, yet flexible, schedule should include time for large and small group work as well as large blocks of time for children to make choices and have experiences in all curriculum areas.

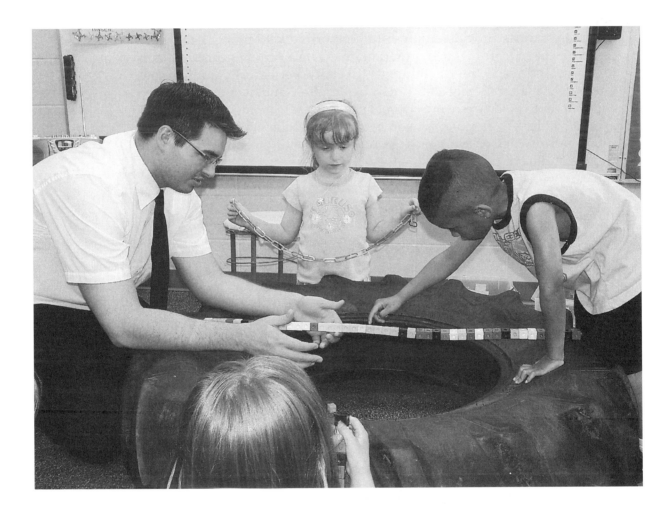

3

Addressing Standards Through Engaging Studies and Authentic Assessment

Standards have assumed an increasingly important role in education over the years. National organizations have developed content standards outlining what children should know and be able to do in each subject area. They serve as a kind of lighthouse to help guide our teaching and illuminate concepts that should be addressed. Most states have also developed their own standards, based on national standards. The Council of Chief States School Officers' Web site provides a link to states' content standards at http://www.ccsso.org/projects/browse_by_topic. Having a copy of the standards our children are expected to meet is a good place to begin our planning.

ENGAGING STUDIES AND PROJECTS

To help children meet standards, we need to intentionally plan experiences that give them opportunities to learn in each of the content areas. Many developmentally appropriate activities, including both child-directed and adult-directed activities, help children meet standards in a whole host of areas. Offering engaging activities with motivating books and hands-on materials helps children work toward meeting standards throughout the day. Long-term studies or projects can provide children with rich learning opportunities in all areas of the curriculum. A *long-term study* or *project* can be defined as an in-depth investigation of a worthwhile topic of interest. Topics for long-term studies ideally come from interests that children have expressed through their play, questions, or conversations. Topics for kindergarten studies should be something children can have firsthand experiences with and be meaningful and relevant to them. It is important to have enough resources and materials for children to fully explore the topic and have many hands-on experiences related to the topic throughout the study.

Science and social studies topics are ideal sources for rich projects that help children learn about and make sense of their world while meeting standards in all areas of the curriculum. As children read and write about their topic, they are learning literacy skills; as they draw and create other representations of what they are learning, they are growing in the arts. Reviewing science and social studies standards can provide us with ideas for topics that would correspond with children's current interests. Life science standards lend themselves to studies of animals and their homes, or specific animals or plants children may be fascinated with, while standards in earth and space science might lead us to studies of rocks or water when we notice how much children are enjoying exploring the rocks we've added to the water table. Children's interest in social studies topics such as maps, clothing, or transportation could also develop into engaging projects.

Project work can be integrated throughout the day. Some of the books we read during our shared literacy time can be related to the topic. Children may choose to write about what they are learning during writers' workshop. Interest areas could be enhanced with topic-related activities and materials. Books about the topic may be added to the library and listening areas. Vocabulary words connected to the topic can be posted, along with corresponding pictures, in the writing area. Enriching the interest areas with project-related materials helps children learn about the topic through a unique lens that each interest area could provide. Studies and projects also provide wonderful opportunities for children to learn new vocabulary as they work and play with topic-related materials, listen to stories, and have rich discussions on the topic.

Children can take part in redesigning the dramatic play area as a place where they can explore the topic even further and represent the knowledge they are learning through their play. If students have been coming to school and talking about stores they have visited to find some of their favorite items, a study of neighborhood stores could help children reach standards in the social studies area of economics as well as many other standard areas. Local stores and families may donate items to enhance the dramatic play area, increasing learning opportunities.

Studies may last for varying amounts of time, depending on the topic and the children's interest. Some may last for a couple of weeks or months, while others could be extended throughout the school year and possibly overlap with other topics. Projects generally begin by asking what questions children have about the topic and what they would like to learn more about. Some teachers like to make a K-W-L chart with their students at the beginning of a study. In a chart divided into three columns, teachers list what the children already know (K) about the topic in the first column, and then in the middle column list what (W) questions or specific areas they would like to pursue. Throughout the study, they revisit the chart to make sure they are addressing all of the questions. At the end of the study, they add information they have learned (L) about their topic to the last column. Many teachers draw a web as they brainstorm with the children the possible areas they would like to investigate. It is helpful to have the chart or web posted where it can be referred to throughout the project.

A long-term project or study has several phases. The first phase introduces the topic and begins the study with brainstorming possible avenues to pursue and questions about the topic. The second phase is when the real investigations take place, including reading about the topic, going on field visits, and gathering information from a variety of other sources. Finally, in the third phase teachers provide opportunities for children to reflect and share the story of all they have learned about the topic.

Phases of Long-Term Studies or Projects

Phase 1. Beginning the Study

- Opening experience or story to kindle additional interest
- Brainstorming with the children possible areas to investigate
- Developing a web or chart with questions or areas related to the topic that children wish to explore

Phase 2. Investigation and Representation: Doing the Actual Work of the Study

- Planning and visiting field sites
- Inviting experts and family members to share information on the topic
- Reading, investigating, and gathering information from a variety of sources
- Playing in interest areas with topic-related materials
- Taking photographs, drawing, dictating, and writing information they have learned
- Documenting children's learning and progress

Phase 3. Concluding the Study

- Completing documentation of the project
- Preparing a culminating event to share the work of the study with others
- Reflecting on what was learned
- Choosing a new topic or direction for the next study or project

---

A study might develop when children begin expressing curiosity about *WET PAINT!* or *DANGER!* signs in the neighborhood. They may express excitement when we point out that they are reading when they correctly identify the *STOP* sign at the corner. Children may be asking to put up signs in the dramatic play or block areas. A study of signs is full of potential for meeting standards in all areas of the curriculum. Children reach standards in language arts as they read and make signs; adding signs to the classroom also provides additional environmental print they can read. Children will be learning health, safety, and science as they discover issues related to warning signs and social studies as they explore signs in the neighborhood. There are many different directions this study could take depending on children's interests, available materials, and your environment.

A Study of Signs

Phase 1. Beginning the Study

- The study might begin with an opening event such as a *sign hunt*, taking a walk around the school with clipboards and pencils, drawing pictures of signs children see, and then discussing what they observed.

- Make a K-W-L chart with the children, listing what they already know about signs and questions they would like to be able to answer.
- Create a web with the children brainstorming possible directions this project could take.

Phase 2. Investigation and Representation: Doing the Actual Work of the Study

- Read Tana Hoban's *I Read Signs* or other books about signs.
- Add props to interest areas:
  - ○ Magnetic letters and numbers for making signs
  - ○ Wooden toy street signs and sign-making material in the block area
  - ○ Books about signs and books with interesting signs to the library and listening areas
  - ○ A variety of paper, cardstock, and washable markers for making signs in the art, writing, and computer areas
- Go on a hunt for signs in the neighborhood or nearby park, clipboards and cameras in hand, noticing colors and shapes.
- Look for signs in buildings, including the school, local grocery, or library.
- Visit a site where a sign is being installed or made by contacting the city or department of transportation.
- Invite someone in to make a sign in the classroom or watch a short video on how signs are made from the Internet, such as that found at www.stopsignsandmore.com.
- Encourage children to make signs for their artwork and block constructions.
- Decide with the children how to transform the dramatic play area, such as changing it into a sign shop, printing shop, or grocery store with many signs.
- Make *EXIT* signs and other functional signs for the classroom and hallways.

Phase 3. Concluding the Study

- Create a class book with children's photographs and other artwork and writing.
- Plan a culminating activity with the children, which might include making a sign museum in the classroom and making signs to invite families and other classes to a gallery opening of the museum. Children could give guided tours and act as tour guides or docents. Wearing a name badge such as "Docent Diego" will add another new word to their vocabulary!
- Celebrate and discuss all that children have learned throughout the study, read the book about signs made by the class, and add to the classroom library.
- Think about new studies the children might be interested in pursuing.

Ask businesses or organizations if they have old posters that could be used during the project to add interest. Although they may not have any on hand, many places would be happy to save posters if they know you are interested. Invite families to bring any signs they may have at home they would like to share, and suggest they discuss signs they see when out with their children.

Try This!

Plan experiences intentionally that help children learn in all areas of the curriculum, including thinking and problem-solving skills. For example, in a sign study, show children a *PED X-ING* sign or a picture of one from the Internet. Ask children what these words might mean. This provides an opportunity to learn a new word, *pedestrian,* and draw attention to the *-ing* ending for words. Brainstorm ideas with the children about how to make and display a *KINDERGARTEN X-ING* sign in the hallway outside the classroom. Children could suggest similar signs to make for a classroom pet, train set, or for other classrooms or personnel in the school.

The sign study could be incorporated into several different parts of the day. During shared literacy, ask children to notice any signs in books you are reading. Work with small groups and individuals on specific activities related to signs during interest-area time. Children can be making signs for many of the activities they are involved in, such as making signs for use in a puppet show. The block area could become a town with many signs that designate places such as a zoo, post office, streets, or highways.

Activities related to signs may also be incorporated into math and science. Extend the learning by taking a walk outside where children can draw and photograph shapes of signs they observe. Set up centers during math and science explorations time to help children meet a variety of math standards by giving them opportunities for several activities, such as classifying and sorting signs by shapes as octagons, triangles, and rectangles; measuring signs; and making patterns with signs.

Try This!

To meet standards in the area of measurement, help children make signs that describe the distance from one point to another. Ask children what distances they would be interested in measuring and what they would like to use to measure the distance. This might include meter sticks, rulers, and nonstandard units of measure, such as blocks, plastic links, or shoes. Work with children in small groups to measure and make arrow signs. A sign for the door might read, *Library—50 meters* or *Block area—14 feet.*

A sign study could last for months or even for an entire year if children's motivation and interest remain high. It could evolve into other topics but remain a thread that would carry throughout other studies. Once children have gotten into the habit of making signs, they can continue doing so even after they have moved onto other investigations.

ASSESSING CHILDREN'S PROGRESS TOWARD REACHING STANDARDS

In order to help children meet standards, it is important to know what standards or goals children need to meet and then regularly assess to know where they are and support their progress. It is important that this be done in developmentally appropriate ways, including observation, portfolios, and checklists.

What Research and the Experts Tell Us

Vygotsky (1978) talked about the importance of assessment to know each child's *Zone of Proximal Development*, which can be described as the distance between what a child is capable of doing independently and what he or she can do with assistance (Bodrova & Leong, 1996). Vygotsky believed that this *zone* is where all learning occurs, just beyond what a child can do alone. When we assess children, we find out what they know and then *scaffold* them to the next level. *Developmentally Appropriate Practice in Early Childhood Programs* (2009) outlines appropriate assessment for kindergarten children, emphasizing that assessment should address all subjects and areas of development. Assessment needs to happen throughout the year and should guide our planning for each child. To be developmentally appropriate, teachers use a variety of methods, including observation and collecting samples of children's work. Teachers gain additional information from families and respectfully share assessment results with them. They collaborate with families to set goals and help children reach them.

Standards provide us with goals children need to achieve. Printing a list of standards in each subject area helps to keep these goals in front of us. A good way to document that we have addressed each of the standards is to put a date next to the standard when we have included it in our teaching. Although touching on a standard once is certainly not enough, this provides helpful documentation for administrators and parents and informs us about topics that need further attention. Standards can also be used to help us develop checklists with skills and understandings we want to be sure each child has acquired.

Observing and Documenting Children's Progress

Observations are a developmentally appropriate way to assess children's progress in meeting kindergarten standards. Observations should be made throughout the day as children play, interact with each other, and work in interest areas. Observations could be recorded in a variety of ways. Use a clipboard or folder with a form for each child that includes areas you need to document. Forms could also be specific to each curriculum area, divided into rows or sections for each child. Some skills are easy to record on a simple checklist, such as letter and sound identification. Other areas specified in the standards may require writing anecdotal records of what you observe children doing and saying. For example, to document science-as-inquiry standards, record observations of children at play in the water table and the science/discovery area. Write down conversations that provide insight into their understanding, such as the following student comments: "Why does my shadow look so long? Can I make it look shorter by moving over here? I'll check it again when we come outside this afternoon and see if it looks the same." These written records provide pieces of concrete evidence that helps document children's progress.

Assembling portfolios of each child's work provides additional documentation of their current skills and understandings, as well as their growth over the course of the year. Collecting purposeful samples of children's work can provide us with a developmentally appropriate way to gain a clear picture of what they are able to do. These work samples provide us with an *authentic assessment* when they are collected as part of children's involvement in meaningful activities that relate to real-life situations where children will actually be using the skill. Asking a child to write a thank you note to a recent visitor is an example of authentic assessment that would give us a sample of a child's writing abilities.

Contents of portfolios could include children's writing, artwork, photographs of their constructions or other work, and video or audio recordings. Involving children in choosing what pieces to put into their individual portfolios helps them become more aware of the learning process and what areas they could work on. Children also enjoy using a date stamp to mark the date on their work. Look at the standards children need to meet and think of work samples that could be collected as evidence to document children's progress and current knowledge. Standards addressed by the work samples may be written on the back of the items.

SUPPORTING CHILDREN LEARNING ENGLISH AS A NEW LANGUAGE

Long-term investigations provide children with a way to learn language in a meaningful context. When children are engaged in a study they find intriguing, they are able to learn new vocabulary because they are immersed in rich words associated with the topic. In a study of signs, children may be learning words, such as *sign, direction, arrow, crossing, metal,* and *stop.* When a new project begins, they are able to learn additional terms connected to that topic. Using many visuals and hands-on materials that involve multiple senses reinforces their language acquisition.

When assessing children who are learning English as a new language, strive to accurately document children's knowledge, not allowing their lack of English vocabulary to mask the knowledge and skills they have. Using a variety of appropriate assessments, including observations and portfolios, helps us gain a true picture of their understanding and enables us to help them progress.

WORKING WITH CHILDREN'S INDIVIDUAL NEEDS

Projects and studies enable children to work at their individual levels. While children are engaged in project work and activities in interest areas, we are able to work with them individually and in small groups, targeting their specific needs. Make any adaptations that children with physical or academic challenges may need to become involved in project-related activities.

Studies are an ideal way for children to express and develop special talents they may have. They can pursue specific areas of interest related to the study topic or investigate an additional topic with our support. To extend their learning, provide additional materials they can use to write stories, create art, and do problem solving and exploration in math and science. Children may also enjoy taking home additional books to further explore their topic.

Developmentally appropriate assessment helps us to know what difficulties children may be experiencing in making progress toward meeting standards and, therefore, guide us to steps we can take to help them. Taking time to work with children individually and in small groups with engaging hands-on materials that hold their interest will help to scaffold their learning. When assessments indicate that children have met expectations, look for new ways to expand their knowledge and understanding with supplementary materials and activities, such as added visits to the school library which will enable them to continue to grow.

Summary

Content standards outline the knowledge and skills children are expected to know and be able to do. There are many developmentally appropriate ways for children to meet standards, including both child-directed and teacher-directed activities. Long-term studies and projects with science and social studies themes provide opportunities for children to learn more about their world and meet standards in each subject area. Assessing children's progress helps to guide our work by informing us about what they already know and what they still need to learn. Assessment should be done in developmentally appropriate ways, while children are engaged in play and meaningful activities through observation, checklists, portfolios, and other authentic documentation.

Nurturing Children's Sense of Wonder Through Science

Incorporating science into our curriculum may provide opportunities for children to gain an appreciation and respect for nature and a genuine sense of wonder. Science is a wonderful gateway for children to discover more about the world and their place in it. Extending our classrooms to include the outdoors opens up new possibilities and opportunities for children to learn. Science can be part of our everyday activities as we encourage children to ask and find answers to their questions, observe the world around them, and play with engaging hands-on materials.

DESIGNING THE ENVIRONMENT TO PROMOTE SCIENCE INQUIRY

Thoughtful consideration of how to incorporate science into the design of our space has a major impact on the way children perceive science and their ability to carry out scientific explorations. Creating a science/discovery area where children are able to observe natural materials and carry out simple experiments can convey to them that science is something they enjoy and do well. A good science/discovery area can be built with the most modest budgets. Many of our own schools, neighboring high schools, colleges, museums, or other community resource centers may have useful science equipment and materials they would be happy to donate or lend. Some possible materials to add to an engaging science/ discovery area include magnifiers, a children's microscope, magnets, prisms, kaleidoscopes, and a balance scale. Enhance the area with science-related books and a CD player with music that includes environmental sounds, such as the seashore.

Think about the outdoor environment as part of your science classroom to increase science concepts children can be learning. A small garden plot for planting vegetables and flowers allows children to experience first-hand what living things need to survive. Installing a small water feature adds beauty, serenity, and opportunities to learn about water. Just bringing the water table or a large container of water or sand outside provides possibilities for science discoveries. Magnifiers, child-safe thermometers, and a balance scale can be taken outside for children to use in exploring natural materials. Many activities typically done indoors can be brought outside to add interest and opportunities to learn more about the world. Bring the easel, paints, and other art materials out and encourage children to use nature as an inspiration for their art. Take frequent walks to observe and discuss plants, animals, clouds, and other science-related interests.

ADDRESSING STANDARDS AND DEVELOPING SCIENCE CONCEPTS THROUGH ENGAGING STUDIES AND EXPERIENCES

The National Science Content Standards include the areas

- Science as inquiry
- Physical science
- Life science
- Earth and space science
- Science and technology
- Science in personal and social perspectives
- History and nature of science

Although each area is distinct, there are many overarching concepts that are woven throughout all of them. As children gain skills and concepts in one area, they make connections that help them in their understanding of other areas. Children learn in all of these areas through inviting, developmentally appropriate activities.

Discovering More About Science as Inquiry

When writing the Science Content Standards, the National Committee on Science Education Standards and Assessment noted that it is important to place more emphasis on *inquiry* and understanding concepts, not on simply learning facts. Their goal for children is to be able to carry out and understand scientific inquiry. Help children achieve this goal by giving them opportunities to ask questions, explore to find information related to their questions, and then use the results of their investigations to come up with explanations and possible answers. Support students in the next step of this process by encouraging them to explain to others what they have learned. When provided with these opportunities, children grow in their abilities to plan and conduct simple investigations, using simple equipment and tools to help them.

Opportunities for Authentic Assessment

Keep anecdotal records of questions children ask that demonstrate their sense of inquiry. Set up engaging investigations, listen, write down children's conversations as they explore, and join in the dialog. Can they suggest possible ways to find answers to questions? After trying out a solution, can they describe what they observed and provide a possible explanation for the results? Continue to set up explorations and scaffold this thinking.

Try This!

Create individual science journals where children record their questions, observations, and findings throughout the year. These may be inexpensive spiral notebooks, two-pocket folders, or paper held together simply with a metal ring and a cardstock cover. Occasionally provide recording forms that children can use and include in their journals. Such forms might include the heading "My Science Report" with half of the page devoted to the subheading "What I Predict" and the other half to "What I See."

A Study of Tools

Long-term studies and projects involving any meaningful science-related topic helps children grow in their sense of inquiry. In a study, children investigate to find answers to questions they have about the topic. Science topics offer a wonderful springboard for these investigations. A study of tools would especially lend itself to helping children learn more about using the *tools of inquiry*. After finding out what questions children have about tools, try asking them what they know about tools that scientists use to help them in their work. Talk about tools that could be put at the science/discovery area, such as magnifiers, binoculars, microscopes, and flashlights to help us see better, a balance scale to compare weights, and thermometers to help us measure temperature. Brainstorm tools to add to other areas of the room, including writing tools for the writing area, rulers and meter sticks for the math area, as well as a variety of brushes, paper punches, and other art tools in the art area. Visit hardware stores and observe people using tools in a variety of settings, or invite family or community members in to demonstrate how they use tools, including gardening tools, building tools, computers, sewing machines, or die-cut tools. Discuss with the children how to convert the dramatic play area into a place that uses tools. This could be a home setting, tool store, construction site, or possibly a fix-it shop. Families or other community members could donate small appliances that no longer work for children to take apart and put back together with tools. Removing the electrical cord and using safety glasses will help to ensure safety. To end the project, children could display tools they have used and created, along with writing and art they have created during the study.

Children will be learning in all areas of the curriculum during their study as they read and write about tools, think up names and labels for tools they have invented, create art, and develop math skills as they use measuring tools. Children will be learning social studies as we explore tools such as maps, globes, and Global Positioning Systems and talk about people who have invented tools and machines that have helped us throughout history.

Discovering More About Science and Technology

To address the Science and Technology Standard, we need to help children understand that science has helped us solve problems over the years. Scientists have developed *technologies* and tools that have helped us learn far more than we could have without them. A long-term study on tools would be an excellent way to address this standard at the kindergarten level.

One of the technologies or tools that has helped us in our work is the computer. Provide children with opportunities to use computers with quality software, such as *Sammy's Science House.* Help children gain awareness that some things are made by human beings and other things are natural by walking around the school and playground with clipboards and paper that have been divided into two parts, *Found in Nature* and *Made by People.* Suggest that children draw pictures or write the names of objects they discover on their walk and put them in the appropriate column.

Try This!

Provide cameras for children to use as another *tool of inquiry.* There are a wide range of cameras available, including some inexpensive digital cameras made especially for children. Parents may be willing to bring disposable digital cameras as part of their children's school supplies that could be used over the course of the year. Children can take photographs of their investigations and use their photos to help them describe what they were investigating, what they did to answer their questions or solve their problems, and what they discovered through their investigations. As children's skills develop, they can dictate or write simple sentences describing what they did, their results, and conclusions. Assist children in turning their photographs and writing into short books they can read and share with classmates and family. Children could take pictures of objects they find that are made by people and additional photos of things found in nature. The photos could be labeled and made into a book using a photo album or by stapling pages together with a cardstock cover. These books may become part of the science/discovery area where children are able to revisit these concepts and deepen their understanding.

Discovering More About Physical Science

Children love exploring physical science as they learn about motion, properties of objects, light, heat, electricity, and magnetism. They never seem to tire of exploring the room with magnets to find objects that are attracted to them. This activity becomes even more of a learning experience for children when we ask them to make predictions before their explorations and then draw conclusions about what kinds of materials are attracted or not afterwards.

Try This!

Insert a combination of small items that will be attracted by magnets, as well as some that will not be, into a clear plastic bottle and secure the lid. Add the bottles to the science/discovery area and encourage children to use magnets to investigate what happens as they move the magnets around the outside of the bottles. After several days of exploration, add colored water to the bottles and allow investigations to continue. Ask children to suggest other media to use in place of the water, such as sand or cornmeal. Provide paper and pencils in the area so children can record their observations.

Children enjoy learning about the states of matter with experiences such as devising ways to make an ice cube melt as quickly as possible, watching ice melt in the water table, or freezing juice to make popsicles. Children enjoy keeping track of the water level in an *evaporation jar.* Fill a jar to the top with water and ask students to predict what might happen if they left the jar on the window sill. Once a week, check the jar and make a mark with a permanent marker to show the current water level, adding the date next to the line. Children will be fascinated that the volume of water decreases even though no one empties it. Repeated experiences with this type of activity helps children learn about states of matter, the water cycle, and how to do inquiry.

Try This!

An engaging way for children to learn more about states of matter is to build an ice castle in an empty water table or another large container. This can be a cooperative effort involving families. Send a letter home requesting that families work with their children to freeze water in an unbreakable container, such as a whipped topping container or orange juice can, and send it to school on *Ice Castle Day.* In cold climates, children could put containers of water outside to freeze. Problem solve with the children how to best use the ice to form an ice castle, deciding which blocks of ice would be best on the bottom and which would work better toward the top. Children can sprinkle coarse salt on top of each chunk of ice before adding another piece. Talk with them about how the salt begins to melt the ice. Then when another piece of ice is added, the water refreezes and becomes part of the newly added piece of ice, helping it to stick together. Children could use an eye dropper to drip liquid watercolors onto the finished castle. Children will be able to admire their finished product and monitor its change back to a liquid over the course of several days.

Encourage children to explore motion by adding balls, cars, trucks, and other wheeled toys to the block area. Help children use blocks and boards as ramps and levers and investigate questions, such as, *Does the car roll down the ramp faster if the ramp is higher or lower? Do big cars or little cars roll faster?*

To learn about properties of materials, children could go on scavenger hunts to find objects made of particular materials, such as wood, metal, or glass. They could collect objects as they find them, draw pictures of them, or take photographs. These photographs could be made into a class book titled, *What Are Objects Made From?*

Discovering More About Life Science

Investigating living things first-hand is a wonderful way for children to learn about their characteristics and life cycles. Although some schools have regulations against pets, a classroom pet is a wonderful way for children to learn about living things and what they need to survive. Guinea pigs require some work but make good kindergarten pets. As children feed the pet, provide water, and experience the thrill of seeing new babies, they will experience exactly what living things need to survive and the similarity between animal parents and their offspring. Setting up an aquarium or even a fish bowl can help children learn about animals, habitats, and environments.

Another way to bring living things into the classroom is to hatch butterflies from a commercial butterfly garden, which can be purchased inexpensively from many school or science supply companies. There are also kits for hatching tadpoles or ant farms. Families and community members are often willing to bring in and share information about pets or other animals they may have. If possible, children also love learning life science by visiting animals on a farm or in the zoo.

A Study of Birds

A long-term study of plants or animals helps children gain concepts that help them better understand life science, as well as develop skills in all areas of the curriculum. A study of birds can develop into an intriguing project as children brainstorm ways to feed and attract birds. Hanging bird feeders outside the classroom window often results in attracting winged visitors that children can observe. Set up a bird observation area near the window, with binoculars and simple bird identification books. Lois Ehlert's *Feathers for Lunch* provides names and pictures of several common birds children may be able to identify. Add *Charley Harper's ABCs* with beautiful illustrations of birds to add more literacy to the area.

Children could learn about habitats and adaptations by trying to make their own bird nests with soil, sticks, grasses, or other natural material outside or at the science/discovery area. They can make simple feeders by tying a string to a pinecone, spreading with peanut butter or honey, and rolling in bird seed. They could also thread a string through a stale bagel, spread with shortening or honey and then shake in a plastic bag filled with bird seed. Stringing O-shaped cereal onto yarn is another feeder they could make and hang. Children can also see what happens when they try planting the birdseed in soil or on another wet material. Invite a naturalist, ranger, or parent who enjoys bird-watching to share information about birds and tips about how to spot them. They might suggest ideas for making your outdoor environment more inviting for our feathered friends, such as adding a water source and cover birds can use. Organizations such as the

National Wildlife Federation provide a host of suggestions and resources as well. Take walks to neighborhood sites where birds tend to flock: a duck pond, park, nature center, or the backyard of one of your families who has been feeding birds.

Try This!

Turn the dramatic play area into a nature center by bringing a freestanding screen tent into the room and adding materials from the science/discovery area, including magnifiers, binoculars, and natural materials. Create a cozy reading corner in the tent with a sleeping bag, small lawn chairs, and small book rack full of field guides and other nature-related books. The screen tent could also be erected outside with similar materials. A nature center could also be constructed with netting or gauze draped over the area or with a perimeter of large blocks.

Exploring Plants

Children are able to learn a great deal about living things by observing plants outside. Bring magnifiers outside to help children focus their attention on a variety of plant life, including grass, flowers, trees, or other plants you may have in your locality. Talk about similarities and differences in the plants. Take walks in the spring to notice buds and other new life. Photograph the plants and trees as they begin to blossom and throughout the season. Make a graph of plants and animals you see on your hikes.

Give children many experiences with growing plants by including a variety of plants in the classroom, including bulb plants such as narcissus and amaryllis. Add a grow light if the room doesn't get enough sunlight and talk with the children about why adding the light helps the plants.

Planting seeds also allows children to have real-life experiences with the cycle of a plant. Children can learn about the needs of living things as they plant seeds in soil and keep them watered. Measuring and recording plants' growth helps children gain skills in many other areas as well. Involve the children in deciding what types of seeds to plant, where to place them, and in what medium to grow them. Let children try out their suggestions, even if they include growing seeds in sand, flour, sugar, shampoo, or ketchup.

If you are able to get dried corn on a cob, place it on a shallow pan of soil and add water when the soil feels dry. Children will love seeing the individual kernels of corn sprouting.

To help children learn more about the life cycle of plants, make miniature greenhouses to hang in the window. At the science/discovery area, provide small, resealable plastic storage bags, bean seeds, cotton balls, water, eye droppers, green construction paper, and tape. Help small groups or individuals use eye droppers to wet a few cotton balls, place bean seeds on the cotton balls, and put them into a small plastic bag. Encourage children to suggest other seeds to compare as well. To make a greenhouse frame, children can fold construction paper in half and cut out a rectangular window through both thicknesses, slightly smaller than the size of the bag. Children can tape or staple the bag inside the greenhouse frame and decorate it with their names, words, and pictures. Hang the greenhouses on the window where children can watch the seeds sprout over time and record their observations.

Try This!

Make caterpillars from old nylon stockings filled with soil and grass seed like teacher Tammy Rusher does with her children. Set the materials out at the science/discovery area where children can stir grass seed into a container of soil and then transfer the mixture into a nylon stocking. Children can decorate the caterpillar with wiggly eyes, pipe cleaner antennae, or other materials. They could predict how long it will take the grass to sprout, measure and record the length as it grows, and then trim with scissors to give it a haircut. Another option is to plant grass in other containers, such as egg shells or yogurt cups that can be given faces, grow grass "hair," and be trimmed. Ask children to brainstorm other places to try growing grass seeds. It will sprout on many wet surfaces, including sponges.

Discovering More About Earth and Space Science

To learn about earth and space science, children need to discover more about the properties of earth materials, objects in the sky, and changes in the earth and sky. Simply having a water table and sand table in the room or outside where they are able to explore sand and water helps students learn about these earth materials. Add a variety of interesting rocks and shells to the science/discovery area, along with magnifying glasses and a microscope if one is available. Children can sort the rocks according to the type of materials they are made of and by their size, texture, and weight. Provide a balance scale for children to use to compare the weights of the rocks and notice characteristics, such as whether the largest rocks are always the heaviest. Outside, children could also investigate soil, sand, pebbles, and rocks with magnifying glasses and enjoy using a balance scale to compare weights in this environment as well.

While you are outside, talk about the sun and the heat and warmth it provides. Discuss differences children can observe between the day and nighttime sky. Ask children to notice the sky and any clouds they may see. Read *It Looked like Spilt Milk* and provide blue construction paper and white paint for children to create a cloud-like picture. Help them write captions describing their pictures, following the predictable words of the book:

"Sometimes it looked like _____ but it wasn't a _____."

Instead of paint, children could use a small container to mix shaving cream and glue, which could be used to make their cloud pictures.

Read books about the seasons and observe seasonal changes in your own setting or a nearby park or woods. Take time during each season to take walks or field trips with clipboards to notice any changes the new season brings. Bring magnifiers and binoculars to look for footprints, nests, webs, and other evidence of living creatures. Take time on the trip to stop and listen. What do you hear? Make the trip a kind of scavenger hunt with children looking for specific items such as a leaves, twigs, blades of grass, rocks, or something *living* and *nonliving.* While outside, children could also draw pictures of what they are seeing or a sketch of the area in that season. Challenge them to find *evidence* of the particular season they are in. They could also collect this evidence with photographs, which could later be made into a class book depicting changes in the seasons. The book could also highlight changes in clothing children wore on the trips each season.

At the beginning of autumn, go outside and ask each child to adopt a favorite tree. Provide opportunities for children to visit their trees each week and draw a picture of what their trees look like that week, using the colors they observe. Even if the trees in your area don't change color, children could visit their tree occasionally throughout the year, looking in and around their tree for any insects, birds, or other animals that may be there or any other interesting features.

Children can learn about weather by observing daily weather changes. A chart can be used to keep track of these changes by adding a tally mark each day to show the number of sunny, rainy, and cloudy days. At the end of the month, make a graph with the data and then compare one month's graph to the next. Use an easy to read thermometer to collect information on the temperature each day; record and graph this as well.

Children also enjoy playing with their shadows. Take children outside at the beginning of the day to trace their shadows and write their names on them. Go back out toward the end of the day, asking children to put their feet in the same place they were earlier, and again help each other trace their shadows. Do this with other objects, keeping the objects in the same place and tracing their shadows at different times of the day. Engage children in a discussion about why they think the shadows may have changed size.

Discovering More About Science in Personal and Social Perspectives

Through the experiences we provide for children, they can come to realize that people can have a positive influence on their environment. They can discover ways to care for the environment through efforts such as conserving materials, not being wasteful with water, paper, or other materials, reusing materials, recycling, and picking up trash. Read about and celebrate Earth Day and Arbor Day. The Arbor Day Foundation's *Nature Explore* program at www.arborday.org/explore has many resources to enhance your science program.

Involve the children in thinking of ways to make their classroom and school more "green" and environmentally friendly. Could we decorate and set boxes in each of the rooms for paper recycling? Could we talk with local organizations about bringing in recycling containers for cans and plastic bottles? Making recycled paper and crayons is easy to do and provides a great demonstration of how materials can be recycled (directions for this can be found in Chapter 9). Ask families to contribute materials such as fabric, wood scraps, containers, buttons, and other items children can reuse to create collages and other works of art or use creatively in their play.

Developing Healthy Habits

As we help kindergarten children meet the science standard of science in personal and social perspectives, we will also be giving them experiences to learn about basic health and safety practices, how to stay healthy and safe, know who to go to for help, as well as how and when to say no to offers. It is critical that children learn good health habits in kindergarten to build the foundation for a future healthy life.

Transform the dramatic play area into a hospital or doctor's office to allow children additional opportunities to learn about health, germs, and disease prevention. You may be able to get a few props, such as disposable stethoscopes, hospital gowns, and booties from local hospitals, doctors' offices, or family members who may work in a medical related field.

Discovering More About the History and Nature of Science

Throughout history, people have helped to make the world a better place through their scientific discoveries, including medical breakthroughs that have helped us combat disease. Communicate to children that there is still a great deal that people do not know; there is much for the world to learn about many topics, including oceans, space, and health. The way we set up our learning environments and the activities we provide convey to our children that we can all be scientists. All of us are able to observe, discover, ask questions, and find out answers.

Try This!

Set out inviting investigations and experiments for children to explore at the science/discovery area. Provide mess trays or large trays with sides to prevent spills. Help children the first time they do one of the experiments and then leave materials for them to explore. As an extension, ask children to think of other materials or variations they might like to try with the investigation. After children have had the opportunity to thoroughly explore an investigation, provide another experiment for them to try. At the kindergarten level, we want to promote children's inquiry, their ability to predict what might happen, and notice the physical changes they are observing. Then based on their observations, draw conclusions about what might happen in the future in similar situations.

Investigation 1

Pour ½ cup milk into a pie pan

Add a few drops of liquid water color, using different colors

Squeeze dishwashing liquid around the side of the pie pan just above the milk, about ⅓ of the way around the pan

Observe what happens. Why do you think this happened?

Investigation 2

Pour a clear soft drink or seltzer into a see-through cup

Add a few raisins

Observe what happens. Why do you think this happened?

Investigation 3

Add baking soda to vinegar

Observe the reaction.

What other materials could we try?

SUPPORTING CHILDREN LEARNING ENGLISH AS A NEW LANGUAGE

Children enjoy science activities, even if they have limited English proficiency. Science may open the door for some children to make connections between the words being used to describe the science materials they have in their hands and the objects they represent. Make sure there are activities that children can do successfully while they are still learning the language and may be reticent to talk out loud. Taking nature walks and pointing out interesting plants and animals can be a motivating way for children to learn and understand new words in context. Make sure children learning English are near you and can hear and easily take part in any demonstrations or discussions you have. Have children walk and work in pairs, partnering a child learning English with one who speaks it well. Take photographs while on the walk and put these into a book with labels children can revisit time and again to help them learn new words.

WORKING WITH CHILDREN'S INDIVIDUAL NEEDS

Many of the activities that could help children learning English as a new language would also be helpful for children who may be having difficulty learning concepts. Provide additional support for children who are having difficulty comprehending any of the concepts presented. Take time to have back-and-forth conversations with them in the science/discovery area. This will give you insight into their current understandings and possible misconceptions, as well as provide opportunities to work with them individually. Make sure all children can access the science materials and participate fully in outdoor science activities. Use a touch screen or modified keyboard and mouse for children who may have difficulty working with the computer.

Exploring science opens up many possibilities for children who are more advanced or those who may be especially interested in science-related topics. Ask them to make signs for objects that have been collected on a nature walk. Recommend science experiences children can do at home with their families, including visiting museums, visiting parks, taking nature walks, and doing simple experiments. Suggest that they keep a science journal of their experiences and write and draw about what they are learning. Encourage children to think of questions they would like to find answers to or topics they would like to investigate and provide resources to help them carry out their investigations.

Summary

The National Science Content Standards include the areas of science as inquiry, physical science, life science, earth and space science, science and technology, science in personal and social perspectives, and the history and nature of science. Teachers will be helping children learn in all of these areas by providing developmentally appropriate science experiences that allow children to explore and investigate a wide variety of materials, using tools that support their inquiry, such as magnifiers and balance scales. Setting up a science/discovery area with interesting supplies and experiments, and enriching the outdoor area to support science learning allows children to explore science throughout the day. Provide experiences that help children learn about plants, animals, and the environment and learn ways to be good stewards of the earth. Studies of science-related topics are an excellent way for children to learn science concepts, as well as skills in all areas of the curriculum. Through science, children can develop a true sense of wonder and joy in learning.

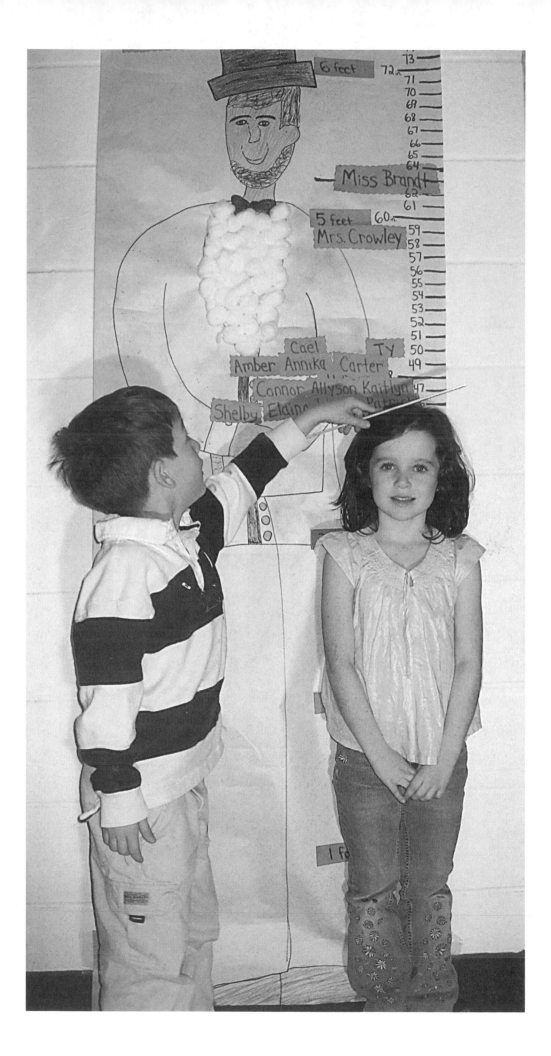

5

Fostering Involved Citizens Through Social Studies

Children will be learning social studies throughout the day as we read books about a variety of cultures, times, and places, vote on a name for a robot they have created, play in the dramatic play area store, and develop into a *community of learners*. Our focus should be on intentionally planning activities that will not only help them meet standards but also to grow to become involved, concerned citizens of our planet. In writing the curriculum standards for social studies, the National Council for the Social Studies described the purpose of social studies as helping students, "make informed and reasoned decisions for the public good as citizens of a culturally diverse democratic society in an interdependent world" (2008, p. 6).

DESIGNING THE ENVIRONMENT FOR OUR FUTURE WORLD CITIZENS

Our room design and materials can help children learn social studies skills and develop positive dispositions that will help them become concerned citizens of our democracy. Hang appealing posters around the room that depict the beauty of various geographic features, such as oceans, mountains, and fields. Other posters should picture children from a variety of cultures and families. Stock the library area with books that feature children from a variety of family structures, cultures, times, and locations. Include simple biographies of men and women who made a difference throughout history. Make sure dolls, puzzles, and other materials represent various races. Include instruments and music from other cultures, such as Dan Zanes' ¡*Nueva York!* and *World Playground: A Musical Adventure for Kids.*

Change props in the dramatic play area to represent various places in the community, which could include a doctor's office or restaurant. Add fabrics and clothing from a variety of cultures and uniforms or props that children can use as they try on pretend roles, such as community helpers.

ADDRESSING STANDARDS AND DEVELOPING SOCIAL STUDIES CONCEPTS THROUGH ENGAGING STUDIES AND EXPERIENCES

There are many experiences we can offer children throughout the day to foster the knowledge and understanding children need in the social studies standards areas that include

- History
- Geography
- Economics
- Civics
- Cultures

Engaging projects with social studies related topics such as homes, stores, clothing, transportation, and our community help children meet standards, not only in social studies, but in all areas of the curriculum.

A Study of Homes

One topic that may interest children and help meet standards is homes. You might decide to start an investigation on homes when you see children building home-like structures in the block area or observe a home construction project taking place nearby.

Begin the project by asking children what they know about homes and creating a web with ideas they share. Send letters home informing families about the topic and ask if any of them have expertise they would like to share about building or caring for a home. Include a questionnaire asking about their homes, including questions on the number of windows, doors, or chairs that you could use to make graphs to help meet standards in math.

The block area is a natural place for a study of homes to develop. Add props to the area to enhance children's constructions, including toy people and animals in need of a good home constructed by a kindergartener. Adding fabrics, wallpaper remnants, and cardboard will enhance creativity and possibilities. Add materials that children could use to make signs and labels for the buildings they create. Leaving the structures up for extended periods of time will lead to more elaborate structures. When it is time to take the structures down, help children take photographs and dictate or write information about their buildings to document what they have done.

Take walks around the neighborhood, clipboards in hand, and ask children to observe different features of the homes each time. If possible, take walks around the neighborhood or to a nearby park to observe animal homes, which might range from dog houses to ant hills, bird nests, and gopher holes.

If you have a home building supply store in the area, arrange a trip or invite one of their staff to come to your classroom with materials. Talk with store personnel in advance to describe what the children have been working on and what they might like to see.

Provide a variety of materials in the classroom that children can use to represent what they have observed, such as wood scraps, paint, glue, sand, and clay. Children could make their own blueprints or diagrams and then build structures based on their plans.

Involve families by asking them to work with their children to draw sketches of the outside of their homes, including doors and windows. Later in the project they might try to draw a more detailed sketch of the room where they sleep or other rooms in their homes.

Children will also be learning more about geography when they view pictures of houses in cities, farms, or African deserts. They can learn more about cultures when we read to them about children who live in different types of homes throughout the world. Studying homes throughout our country's past is a great way for them to make meaningful connections to history. Children will be fascinated to see pictures of Thomas Jefferson's home, Monticello, with its trap doors, dumbwaiters, and the beautiful gardens he helped to develop.

Discovering More About History

Help children learn more about history by reading stories about inspirational figures in history, including Abraham Lincoln, Sacagawea, Johnny Appleseed, Amelia Earhart, Martin Luther King Jr., and Barack Obama. Children will gain a better grasp of the past by making simple timelines. This will be even more relevant by helping them make a timeline of their own lives. Take a picture of each of the children, and ask families to send in pictures of them when they were babies, toddlers, and preschoolers. Children could also draw self-portraits of themselves at these ages. Set up a history center or bulletin board where children could make individual timelines, connecting each of their pictures with ribbon or yarn and include descriptive labels.

Make a class timeline on one of your walls, beginning with a picture of the class on the first day of school. Continue to add pictures and dates throughout the year of the class involved in interesting studies or events. This could be placed above a long strip of paper where you keep track of the number of days in kindergarten, adding one number each school day, making this more meaningful as well.

Discovering More About Geography

Stock the library area with colorful picture books that will give children a look at the variety of geographic aspects of the earth. Talk about our world's natural resources and discuss why it is important for us to have clean water and air, trees, and soil. Brainstorm ways to be good stewards of our environment, such as picking up our trash and turning off water and lights when we are finished with them. Download the free software program *Google Earth* onto your computer, which will allow you to zoom into your state, city, neighborhood, and even school address. Once you have shown children where they are located, zoom back out and show where they are located in relationship to other areas.

A long-term project on maps provides opportunities for children to learn many geography skills. Children love to make treasure maps and can begin making maps of their classroom, school, and playground. Go outside with clipboards and paper and invite children to make a map of the area around the school. Write out simple directions for the children to follow. Hang maps of local areas, the country, and the world around the room and place a globe where children can examine it. Talk about what the blue area represents on maps and globes and encourage children to add areas of both land and water to the maps they are making.

Opportunities for Authentic Assessment

Invite children to make three dimensional maps in the block area using a large sheet of paper, along with blocks, milk cartons, or other materials. Ask them to describe their maps, including bodies of water, houses, streets, or other features.

Try This!

Find out what countries the families of your students, or their ancestors, came from originally. Mark these on an easy to read map or globe, along with your location, using sticky dots or pennant-shaped stickers. Read books about a variety of countries and mark these on the map with a different type of sticker or use a different map or globe for your book travels.

Discovering More About Economics

Children will learn a great deal about economics by setting up a store in the classroom. This could be in the context of a study of stores, community helpers, and the neighborhood or simply as a fun learning activity. Children could choose the type of store to create, such as a toy store, grocery store, shoe store, or clothing store. You could also start with one type of store and change to another to keep children interested and motivated. Each transformation provides opportunities for children to learn new vocabulary associated with that particular type of store.

Try This!

Assisting children in creating their own currency will teach them a great deal about the basics of economics. They may come up with a name like *kindergarten cash*. Their currency could contain a *1-kindergarten cash* bill, which could be green with a large numeral *one* written on it and a *10-kindergarten cash* bill, which might be yellow with the numeral *10* featured prominently. Children could also use a specific rubber stamp picture for each denomination. The math area could become the classroom *mint* where children could produce the *cash*. Items in the store they display could be priced in *kindergarten cash* and children could make price tags. A toy cash register or one made from a box could hold the *cash*. This is a fun way for children to learn more about economics, math, phonemic awareness, and more!

To further their knowledge of economics, children could make items to sell at their store, including beaded bracelets, pencil toppers with silk flowers, or bags of snack mixes. The art area could become a production area where children decorate small notebooks, grocery lists, wrapping paper, and gift cards. Set up a recycling center near the art area where children could put their paper scraps, which could be reused or made into recycled paper to use or sell, helping children see another cycle of goods and services.

Talk with children about the difference between *needs* and *wants*. Provide magazines in the art area children can use to cut out pictures of things they need and things they want. They can glue their pictures onto paper folded in half with the words *needs* and *wants* at the top of each section. This will help you assess children's knowledge of these concepts.

Introduce children to the concept of community helpers and invite family members to come in and share information about their occupation. Visit local community helpers in your neighborhood. Children could try out the role of shopkeeper and learn more about this occupation when the dramatic play area is set up as a store. They will learn about other occupations when the props in the dramatic play area change to become a hospital, doctor's office, fire station, or other places in the community.

Discovering More About Civics

Help children grow in their understanding of community by working to create a community in the classroom. What can we do to make this the best community it can be? Ask children to help you create a job chart with tasks that need to be done in order to make the classroom run more smoothly. Depending on your classroom, this could include watering plants, feeding pets, holding the door, or delivering messages. This is one way to begin helping children develop responsibility and leadership skills. Children could also help you designate roles such as shoe-tying helper, coat-zipping assistant, computer aide, or cleanup partner to encourage children to take a leadership role in helping each other. Talk with children about wanting to have a community where everyone is equal and has opportunities, explaining that this is one reason we share jobs like line leader, so that everyone can have a turn.

Have class meetings and discuss upcoming events or issues that might have emerged. Talk about what a citizen is and discuss characteristics that would make a good kindergarten citizen, including honesty, helpfulness, kindness, and trying your best. Discuss the fact that it isn't always easy to be a good citizen but we can always keep trying. Read stories about Martin Luther King Jr. and other role models, pointing out the fact that they continued to try, in spite of the obstacles they had to face. Involve children in doing something to help the community, such as conducting a food or school supply drive or drawing pictures for the elderly or children in the hospital.

A very concrete way for children to experience civics is to be involved in making rules for the classroom. In their *Songs of Resilience,* the Devereux Institute suggests three simple rules that children can easily remember, especially after listening to the song several times:

1. Take care of myself

2. Take care of my friends

3. Take care of my school

Children may decide they would like to adopt these as their classroom rules just as they are or help compose their own version.

Provide opportunities for children to experience democracy in action by voting. They might vote to decide on what to title a class book, what color to make the play dough, or what song they would like to sing. Add mathematics to this civics activity by making a graph to display the results of the vote.

Discovering More About Cultures and Families

Read books that portray a variety of family structures, making sure that all of our children feel that their family structures have value. Brainstorm benefits of being part of a family and talk about how to be good members of our families. Help children develop an appreciation for people from diverse cultures and backgrounds. Read books reflecting a variety of cultures and families, making sure they include pictures of children in current times, such as *Children of Native America Today.*

Try This!

Read *It's Okay to be Different* by Todd Parr or other books that celebrate our similarities and differences. Kindergarten children especially enjoy reading *We Are All Alike... We Are All Different* written by kindergarteners. Brainstorm a list of characteristics all of us share (we all have eyes, can smile, like to play) and ways people can differ (different eye and skin color, like to play different things). Children could then each make their own pages for a class book, with words such as, "*We all have eyes, but our eyes can be different,*" or "*It's okay to have...*". Read the book to your children throughout the year and add it to your class library so children are able to revisit it often.

Long-term studies or projects related to clothing, food, homes, or transportation provide opportunities to explore the experiences of children in other countries or cultures related to these topics. Play songs from a variety of cultures to help children appreciate the beauty of this music. This is also a wonderful way for children to begin to learn another language, as they repeatedly listen to words on a favorite album, such as Ella Jenkin's *Sharing Cultures.*

Get to know the families of your children and invite them in to share aspects of their family background and customs, including dress, language, traditions, and favorite family recipes. Invite parents to come in to prepare or share some of these recipes with the children.

Try This!

Recipe for Tortillas

Assist children in mixing	Add	Allow children to knead their own ball of dough and roll out; then have an adult cook in a skillet. Provide healthy toppings to add, such as cheese and tomatoes.
1 cup flour	⅓ cup warm milk	
½ teaspoon salt	Divide into six or seven balls	
½ teaspoon baking powder		
1 tablespoon shortening		

Celebrate holidays and special days from many cultures, especially those that your children's families recognize. Invite them in to share special aspects of their celebrations with the class. Heifer International (http://www.heifer.org), Teaching Tolerance (http://www.teachingtolerance.org), and other organizations have free materials they are happy to provide for teachers that can help children gain a deeper understanding and appreciation for others.

SUPPORTING CHILDREN LEARNING ENGLISH AS A NEW LANGUAGE

Studies of familiar topics, such as homes, cars, and clothing provide many opportunities for children to learn common words in context. Make sure to take time to explain the words and concepts you are talking about and use concrete objects and pictures whenever possible. Enhance the dramatic play area with props that relate to the topic you are studying and label them. Take time to play with the children and point out these new objects, repeating their names.

Add books to the library corner that have words both in English and another language, such as *Buenas Noches Luna/Good Night Moon*. Provide simple pictures books with labels that deal with topics such as home and transportation. Invite community members who speak the languages of the children to come on field trips and into the classroom occasionally to help translate words relating to what you are currently studying.

WORKING WITH CHILDREN'S INDIVIDUAL NEEDS

Being involved in engaging studies involving topics children can relate to easily, such as families and homes, make concepts easier for children to understand. Find out what children are especially interested in and integrate that into other learning to gain and keep their attention. If a child has a special interest in trains, provide simple books about trains, train-shaped paper for writing and painting, and use toy trains to illustrate beginning geography concepts such as over, under, near, far, left, and right.

Ensure that all materials are accessible to children with special needs. Visit field sites ahead of time to see if there are special accommodations that need to be made. Make sure dolls, posters, and books in the room are representative of a variety of abilities, including children in wheelchairs, wearing glasses, hearing aids, or other assistive devices. Encourage children to do daily routines and jobs with a partner.

For children who have already achieved needed skills, challenge them by offering more advanced books on topics you are studying. Provide resources to help them learn more about a new culture or language. Children who could benefit from additional challenges might enjoy learning about children in another country or a historical figure of interest. They could look at books or Web sites on their interests, draw pictures, and make a book that they could share with others.

Summary

Children can meet the social studies standards of history, geography, economics, civics, and cultures and families through daily experiences in the classroom, such as reading books about a variety of people, places, and times, opportunities to take part in voting on classroom issues, and taking responsibility for helping with jobs around the room. Teachers can use the social studies standards as a springboard to find topics for engaging projects and studies that will help children meet standards in all areas of the curriculum. Topics such as homes, families, clothing, food, and our community provide many opportunities for children to learn social studies skills. Teachers can enhance the room with posters, books, dolls, fabrics, instruments, and music from a variety of cultures and invite families in to share customs and traditions. Intentionally planning activities that give children rich experiences in all aspects of social studies can help children develop skills and dispositions they will need to become engaged citizens.

Engaging Young Readers and Writers in the Literacy-Rich Kindergarten

Helping children along the road to becoming readers and writers is a very important part of our work in kindergarten. Being able to make sense of the printed word and communicate one's thoughts through spoken and written words opens up an exciting new world for children. The entire kindergarten day offers opportunities to help children in their language and literacy acquisition. It is important to intentionally think about how to make the best use of these opportunities.

DESIGNING A NURTURING ENVIRONMENT FOR YOUNG READERS AND WRITERS

Carefully planning the room design will expand the potential for literacy learning. Our room can promote language and literacy through books, posters, signs, and charts hanging on the wall. Offering a comfortable library/reading area where children look forward to cuddling up with a good book is a great way to begin. The area might include a rug, floor pillows, bean bag chairs, and washable stuffed animals or story book characters from favorite books, such as *Madeline, Dora,* or *Spot.* Make sure to have a variety of genres including fiction, nonfiction, and poetry, and a variety of topics that appeal to both boys and girls and a multitude of interests. Rotate books to fit with the topics you are currently investigating. Children also enjoy reading books made by the class and benefit from revisiting them often in the library area.

A listening area where children can listen to audio books is a wonderful way to increase the amount of books children hear. Teachers often say that they wish they could clone themselves to be able to get more done. Recording a book on tape or CD with the help

of children is one way to come close to doing that; children can listen to you reading while you're busy working with another group across the room! Children would relish the opportunity to help you make the recording by assisting in making the signal to indicate that it's time to turn the page using a xylophone, bell, or other sound, and could join in repetitive refrains. Families might be willing to make these as well.

Introducing a writing area to the room encourages children to spend time writing stories, books, and letters. As with so many other skills, the more time they spend writing, the better their skills become. The writing area could be located on any available table or place where a few children can gather to write. Some teachers bring in a couple of desks from another room and place them facing each other to form their writing area. You could even use floor pillows and lap desks or clipboards. Occasionally, add additional writing surfaces, such as small chalk boards, white boards, or a magnetic writing board. Vary the writing materials from time to time with fun-colored pencils, rubber alphabet stamps with washable inkpads, interesting notebooks, and note cards. This area could be located near a word wall so children could use words posted there.

Try This!

Scan your outdoor environment to see if there is a spot to set up a writing nook where several children could write using clipboards while sitting on small benches or plastic milk crates. A cozy reading area could also be incorporated outside with the addition of some good books, outdoor pillows, a thick blanket, sleeping bag, or small plastic swimming pool. A small see-through screen tent could enclose all this if you have one available to make this area more special.

Think about ways to add literacy to all parts of your room. Enhance the math and science areas with interesting math and science books, writing materials, and graphs the class has made. Post words to songs, poems, and chants, and point to the words when you use them. Boost the literacy potential in the block area with signs, sign-making materials, blueprints, and maps.

Try This!

Decorate a box and fill it with a variety of fun glasses and pointers children can use to *Read the Room* during interest-area time. Children can choose a pair of glasses and a pointer to search the room for posters, charts, word walls, or any other print to read. Pointers can simply be artificial flowers, back scratchers, rulers, or even a flashlight! Plastic glasses can be purchased inexpensively or children can decorate glasses made from paper towel rolls. Another box or plastic tub can hold clipboards, pencils, washable markers, and paper for children to *Write the Room,* with the invitation to write any of the print they find around the room. Occasionally, decorate the pointers, writing materials, or clipboards to go along with a topic you're currently studying to increase children's interest in the activity.

What Research and the Experts Tell Us

There are many strands of skills and knowledge children need in order to become successful readers and writers. Children need strong background knowledge, good vocabulary, concepts about print, phonological awareness, understanding of the alphabetic principle, letter-sound correspondence, and sight recognition of familiar words. Along with these skills, children need to be able to comprehend and understand what they read, have good fluency, and have interest and motivation to read for multiple purposes. The National Research Council report, *Starting Out Right* (Burns, Griffin, & Snow, 1999) states that children who get off to a good start in reading and writing tend to continue to do well. Children who have difficulty early on tend to continue to have trouble unless they receive effective intervention. It is imperative in kindergarten that we help children get off to a good start. To get this positive start, children need to experience enthusiasm, joy, and success in their early efforts at learning to read and write (Burns et al., 1999; Dickinson & Neuman, 2007; Snow, Griffin, & Burns, 2005).

The National Council of Teachers of English and the International Reading Association have outlined standards for students to achieve by the time they have completed 12th grade (http://www.ncte.org/standards). Most states have also developed standards in the language arts, primarily revolving around the areas of reading, writing, listening, and speaking.

In their document, *Learning to Read and Write: Developmentally Appropriate Practices for Young Children*, the National Association for the Education of Young Children (NAEYC) and the International Reading Association (IRA) have outlined goals for preschool through the primary grades as part of a continuum of children's development in reading and writing. They list seven goals for kindergarten.

Kindergarteners can

1. Enjoy being read to and themselves retell simple narrative stories or informational texts

2. Use descriptive language to explain and explore

3. Recognize letters and letter-sound matches

4. Show familiarity with rhyming and beginning sounds

5. Understand left-to-right and top-to-bottom orientation and familiar concepts of print

6. Match spoken words with written ones

7. Begin to write letters of the alphabet and some high frequency words

(Neuman, Copple, & Bredekamp, 2000)

The remainder of this chapter provides suggestions for helping children meet these goals. Teachers need to intentionally plan experiences that not only help children acquire the skills that research has shown to be necessary in order to become successful readers and writers, but also develop a love of books and reading. It is important to know each child's current skills and provide the support she or he needs to experience success as each continues to develop language and literacy skills.

Opportunities for Authentic Assessment

Make a checklist with the NAEYC/IRA goals listed above or your own state standards and ask children to demonstrate these skills in meaningful situations. While others are engaged in interest areas and literacy centers, ask individuals to read simple, repetitive books to you. Use leveled books if they are available. Ask individuals to point out familiar concepts of print in a book as you read and then ask them to retell the story. Encourage them to find rhymes and words that begin with the same sound as their names and mark their accomplishments on the checklist.

ADDRESSING LANGUAGE AND LITERACY STANDARDS AND GOALS THROUGH ENGAGING STUDIES AND EXPERIENCES

Language and literacy can be incorporated throughout the day from the moment children enter the classroom. Greeting the children as they arrive and engaging them in conversation builds language skills. This also helps them start their day with a positive attitude toward themselves and the day of learning ahead. Literacy continues as children sign-in each day. This can be done by inviting children to sign in on a piece of paper during your welcoming time. Daily sign-in sheets will give you an authentic documentation of children's growth over the year as you compare their first signatures with those later in the year.

GOAL—Kindergarteners can enjoy being read to and themselves retell simple narrative stories or informational texts.

Offering a *shared literacy time* after children have had a chance to settle in provides a wealth of opportunities for growth in language and literacy. Begin shared literacy time with a favorite song and ask that children join you in the meeting area by the time the song is over (Fisher & Medvic, 2000). Greet children as they join you with a simple written message on the board or a chart including information about the events of the day. Use a predictable pattern with sight words that children will begin to recognize, such as:

> *Today is* _____ (insert day of the week)
>
> *We will go to* _____ (insert special activities such as the *library, apple orchard, or assembly*)
>
> *We will have fun!*

Continue shared literacy time by reading a familiar big book. According to the National Commission on Reading (Anderson, Hiebert, Scott, & Wilkinson, 1985), "The single most important activity for building the knowledge required for eventual success in reading is reading aloud to children" (p. 23). A special helper of the day might choose a favorite big book and song. Shared reading boosts children's confidence to read with their peers and join in as they are able. Reading familiar big books with predictable text increases children's *fluency*, which is one of the skills research has found to be

essential to becoming a successful reader. Choose quality books with only a small amount of text on each page and appealing pictures that complement the words, such as *It Looked like Spilt Milk*. Cultivate fluency by using books with words to familiar songs that children can sing along with as you turn the pages.

Try This!

Write out words to favorite songs on a large chart. Point to the words as the children sing them. Later in the year, invite children to point to the words with appealing pointers as the words are sung. Use highlighting tape to draw attention to sight words that are helpful for children to know. Making one chart each quarter will give you four new charts each year. You can store charts with songs, poems, and chants by folding the edges of the chart paper over the sides of a hanger and taping in place. The charts can be hung and stored easily.

Each week, introduce a new big book at shared literacy time after children have enjoyed reading a familiar book. Choose an informational book that goes along with a topic you are studying or a book that provides good models of concepts or letters you want students to learn. Shared reading with big books provides a meaningful context for purposefully teaching children literacy strategies. To build *comprehension* skills, ask children to predict what a book might be about before reading and then see if their predictions are accurate as you read. After reading the book, ask children to retell the story in their own words. Make story charts on the board with three sections—beginning, middle, and end, allowing children to help you draw and write about what happened at these points in the story. Children can do these on their own later in the year at the listening area.

Comprehension and retelling skills will also be strengthened by suggesting that children act out a story after reading. Children will enjoy retelling stories with puppets, flannel board characters, and other props. Reading with expression and using amusing voices for characters in the stories will enhance children's motivation and attention, and will also help them comprehend the stories they hear. Encourage children to create voices for some of the characters in the stories and use them as you read the book. They can also use these voices in their retellings.

End shared literacy time with another song accompanied by some movement to keep children actively engaged. Shared literacy time not only helps children build critical literacy skills but it also promotes a sense of community as children read and sing together and see themselves as active participants in the community of readers and writers.

GOAL—Kindergarteners can use descriptive language to explain and explore.

Developing language skills assists children in acquiring other literacy skills as well. Children from impoverished homes come to school knowing far fewer words than their peers (Hart & Risley, 2003). It is important that our kindergartens provide a language-rich experience for all of our children through discussions, conversations, and many opportunities to listen to stories. Reading to children enriches their *vocabularies*, a critical building block on the road to successful reading and writing.

Projects or themes provide opportunities for children to learn words in context as they investigate and learn new words and concepts associated with the topics. For example, in a study of signs, children can read signs around the room and their neighborhoods and begin to notice more of the environmental print around them. Have a special Wear a Sign day; then make a graph showing how many came with words on their shirts, caps, or shoes. Children might have the chance to watch a sign maker create a sign providing motivation for them to make their own signs.

Take advantage of free time outside, interest-area time, and mealtime to engage children in conversation. Individual conversations with caring adults are one of the best ways for children to enhance their language as well as *knowledge about the world*, another key component necessary to becoming a successful reader and writer.

Try This!

Involve families by asking them to send something to school with print that their child can read, such as the front of a favorite cereal box or packaging from a toy. Punch holes and bind the printed materials together with ribbon, yarn, or binder rings to assemble into a book. This will be a favorite choice to read with a friend in the library area!

GOAL—Kindergarteners can recognize letters and letter-sound matches.

Make opportunities for children to learn letters and sounds in meaningful contexts throughout the day, pointing out key letters and sounds in big books and song charts. Using children's names is a powerful way to help them learn the alphabet and literacy skills. Talk with children about the letters in their names and the sounds the letters make. Once they can identify and have made the letter-sound connection with these letters, it will be easier for them to broaden this knowledge to other letters. Set up centers during interest-area time where children could write their names with a variety of materials as well as alphabet centers with a variety of activities children can choose from that change over time:

- Alphabet stamps with washable stamp pads
- Alphabet puzzles and books
- Alphabet cookie cutters and play dough
- Alphabet beads, blocks, letter tiles, and magnetic letters
- Pocket chart with alphabet letters and pictures children can match with beginning sounds
- Overhead projector with letters

As children become more familiar with the alphabet, encourage them to make simple words. Provide opportunities that will help children learn sight words, rhyming words, and beginning and ending sounds in words, including playing matching games with words on file cards.

Play games to increase children's alphabet knowledge both inside and outdoors. Distribute cards with a capital letter to half of the children and cards with the corresponding lowercase letters to the other half. Challenge children to find their classmates with the matching letter. Have scavenger hunts for objects beginning with different letters.

Try This!

Set up a center where children can use alphabet beads to make name bracelets or necklaces. Later in the year, they can use the beads to create bracelets with sight words. Bracelets could also be made with a strip of construction paper or other heavy paper. Children could stamp or write a sight word on bracelets to wear and share what they've learned with their families.

Providing fun experiences with letters and sounds helps children understand the *alphabetic principle* and make letter sound connections so necessary to becoming successful readers and writers. Take advantage of opportunities throughout the day to use the alphabet and highlight letters and sounds in the context of daily activities. The National Research Council (Burns et al., 1999) recommends that we help children appreciate the *beauty* of the alphabet. Reading engaging alphabet books both boys and girls will enjoy, such as *A Child's Day: An Alphabet of Play* can increase children's enjoyment, knowledge, and appreciation.

Try This!

Each time you introduce a sight word, attach a copy of the word to a wooden building block or connecting block. Keep all the sight-word blocks in a container that children can play with and use to form sentences.

GOAL—Kindergarteners can show familiarity with rhyming and beginning sounds.

Being able to rhyme and identify beginning sounds in words will help children develop *phonological awareness,* another key ingredient in learning how to read and write. Ask children to think of words that begin with the same sound as their names and make rhymes. Sing rhyming songs with their names, such as *Willoughby Wallaby Woo* and the *Name Game.* Make class books using the children's names. After reading books such as *Baby Bear, Baby Bear, What Do You See?,* set up a writing center where children can dictate and illustrate a page for a class book using their names, following the pattern found in the books. Xander's page might read, *Xander, Xander, What do you hear? I hear a yellow chick peeping in my ear.* If you have permission from the parents, take photos of the children to put on their pages. After children have completed their pages, make a cover for the book and bind the pages together. Allowing children to take turns taking the book home to read to their families will make this even more effective as a learning tool.

Try This!

Make good use of waiting time by singing rhyming songs or playing games to build phonological awareness. Here's a fun name game kindergarten teacher Roberta Gray's children love and could become part of your daily routine as the class gets ready to go outside each day. Choose a letter and ask children to say their names as if it started with that particular letter. If you've read a book about mice that day, you might choose the letter *M.* Call on children one at a time to say their names and then get ready to go outside. Ella would say *Mella,* and Ava would say *Mava.* Children will improve with practice and later can even work with sounds such as *th* and *br.*

GOAL—Kindergarteners can understand left-to-right and top-to-bottom orientation and familiar concepts of print.

Pointing out features of the books we are reading can help children learn *concepts about print,* including *title, author, and front* of the book. Demonstrate that reading proceeds from *left to right* and *top to bottom* by pointing to words as you read from time to time. Intentionally use terms such as *word, sentence, period,* and *uppercase* and *lowercase letters.*

In her book, *Joyful Learning in Kindergarten,* Bobbie Fisher (1998) recommends "masking" features as we read to help children learn concepts about print. Masking frames could be made from any stiff paper by cutting out an opening that could then be used to frame a specific word or letter. These frames can focus children's attention when we ask them to put frames on certain letters or words. Vary your questions by asking them to frame features such as first words in a sentence, words that rhyme with a given word, and words that begin or end like another word (Fisher & Medvic, 2000).

Try This!

Make masking frames out of a variety of materials, including file cards, cardstock, or envelopes with windows. Cut a hole out of a new fly swatter, or use the top of a pretty facial tissue box. Form masking frames from pipe cleaners or wiki sticks, which can stick right to the page. Highlighter tape can also be purchased at teacher or office supply stores to highlight words and letters.

Making their own books is an enjoyable and effective way for children to learn concepts of print. Children will be putting these concepts into practice as they take part in writing books as a class. After reading books, such as *Have You Seen my Duckling?*, provide a center where children can create their own pages. Include drawing and writing tools, along with blank paper, or paper with words, such as

Have you seen my _____?

Mother _____ said.

Following the predictable pattern of the book, children can write in the name of a baby animal on the top line and its mother on the next line. They could visit the center each day for a week, making a separate page each day and then bind them together. Instead of making individual books, students could each make one page at the center and then combine all their pages to make a single class book, which could be read frequently. Predictable class books can be made with software programs, such as Kid Pix, which allow teachers to create templates that children could use in their writing, and provides opportunities to illustrate using the computer. Templates could also be made with any word processing program.

Try This!

Bind class books with a variety of materials. After adding colorful cardstock or construction paper covers, punch holes and weave yarn or ribbon, or use brass fasteners to secure the pages. Laminating the pages or front and back covers will increase their durability. Class books can be made by slipping pages into inexpensive three-ring binders or photo albums. Books can also be bound with inexpensive plastic comb binding available at print shops.

GOALS—Kindergarteners can match spoken words with written ones and begin to write letters of the alphabet and some high frequency words.

Reading and writing skills strengthen and support each other; as children develop skills in one area, their understanding of the other increases. One of the concepts kindergarten children need to begin to comprehend is the understanding that a symbol can represent something else. This is a concept necessary for advancing understanding in all areas of the curriculum (e.g., a numeral can represent an actual number of objects; a map can represent a community, state, country, etc.). As children become familiar with letter symbols and their sounds, they begin to develop the understanding that those letters can be combined to make words, and that those words can be used to represent actual objects. Taking down children's dictation and reading it back to them helps children begin to grasp this concept. Enlist the help of family members, educational assistants, and older students who could act as "big buddies" to take down children's dictation and read it back with them.

Writers' Workshop Time

Each day, make time for a writers' workshop to provide children with opportunities to learn and practice skills and promote their feelings of belonging to the community of readers and writers.

Shared Writing

Begin writers' workshop by inviting a designated student author for the day to dictate a sentence as you record what the author says. Think out loud as you write, describing your actions. Encourage students to help you sound out words as you write and decide when to use spaces, capitals, and punctuation. Children can become more involved as the year progresses.

Individual Writing Time

Make sure that children have individual writing journals they can use each day. The journal can be a spiral notebook or a two-pocket folder that parents bring as part of the beginning of the year school supplies. Monthly writing journals can be made by stapling sheets of paper together with a motivating cover using a seasonal picture or a set of alphabet letters from the Internet.

After shared writing with the group, ask children to think about what they would like to write in their journals and invite them to find a spot in the room to do their writing. Play a variety of music to add to the atmosphere. Encourage children to write about topics that interest them to provide more motivation for their writing. Children can begin their writing time by drawing pictures. These pictures are an important part of kindergarten writing and can help children develop the details of their stories. Encourage children to write whatever they can to accompany their pictures. As children see writing being modeled and have multiple experiences, they continue to grow in their skills, adding more letters and eventually words. With support, kindergarten children will be able to write simple sentences to go along with their illustrations.

Encouraging children to sound out the letters in the words they want to write can help to strengthen their writing skills. This is commonly referred to as invented, developmental, estimated, or emergent spelling. Several states' kindergarten literacy standards include being able to use emergent spelling as well as beginning to read what they have written (Seefeldt, 2005). The National Research Council (Burns et al., 1999) suggests that invented spelling can help children develop letter-sound-spelling understanding, as well as phoneme identity and segmentation.

Coupled with quality instruction, they believe invented spelling can help children spell and remember words with increasing accuracy. They also recommend that writing take place on a daily basis.

Writing dictionaries can be a helpful tool for children in their writing. There are commercial dictionaries that can be purchased or you can make your own with one letter on each page. Personalize the dictionary with words that fit your school, community, and families. Add children's names to the pages corresponding with the first letters in their names. Waiting a few months before using the dictionary will give children time to develop confidence in sounding out words on their own.

The dictionary could be introduced at parent-teacher conferences after the first quarter. Ask families to add the names of family members, pets, or other important words to their child's dictionary at the end of the conference. The dictionary can then be used throughout the year at writing time to support children's writing. Because it is a dictionary, it is beneficial to have adults write the words in the dictionary to ensure that words are spelled correctly and are easy to read. If done well, the dictionary could be passed on to the first grade classroom or beyond, with a year's worth of words that are meaningful to the child.

Opportunities for Authentic Assessment

Support children's writing by having individual *writing conferences* with them as they write, making sure to talk with each child at some point during the week. During the conferences, ask children to tell you about what they are writing and to read it to you. This will help you assess their current level of writing skills. Scaffold children by suggesting they work on skills just beyond what they are currently doing. Try to have many back-and-forth conversational exchanges during the conference and provide quality feedback that will help them progress.

Storing children's writing in individual portfolios provides authentic assessment and documents children's growth throughout the year. This is also a wonderful way for children to see the progress they have made and can be used as a springboard to talk about what they might work on next to advance their writing even more. You will also be able to show families how much their children have progressed throughout the year and discuss ideas they can work on at home to continue this growth.

Author's Chair

After individual writing time, children can come back together to share their writing. At the beginning of the year, children may only be able to draw and write on their own for about five minutes, but by the end of the year, they might write for 20 to 30 minutes, depending on their interests and motivation. Because children will finish writing at different times, offer an activity they can do when they finish their writing, such as listening to an audio book or looking at books in the library area until individual writing time is finished. Play a designated piece of music or sing a song as a sign that it is time to gather again in the group meeting area for authors' chair. Each day, have three or four children share what they've written, giving them an audience and more motivation for their writing. Children can sign up to be authors and take turns so that each child has the opportunity to share. Encourage children to give compliments to the author by describing something specific about the author's writing that they noticed or appreciated. This boosts self-esteem and provides suggestions other children may be able to incorporate into their own writing.

Try This!

Provide a festive author's chair that will offer additional motivation for children's writing. This could be made from any chair by adding a decorative author's chair sign and ribbons or streamers. The chair could be a rocker, easy chair, tree stump, stool, or other whimsical seating. Children will love being an author and having the opportunity to share their writing in this special chair.

Publishing Children's Writing

Publishing children's writing is another way to motivate children, helps them learn concepts about print, and increases their reading skills. Talk about the process of publishing, including beginning with a draft, editing, and revising to make a final copy. Encourage children to write and illustrate simple stories with a beginning, middle, and end. During individual writing conferences, assist children in editing and revising their stories. When the final copy of their story is finished, encourage children to design a cover on construction paper or cardstock. They could also add a dedication page, including a copyright date and city. Children could number their pages as well, putting math concepts into practice. With assistance, children could also write stories on the computer using software, such as Stanley's Sticker Stories, Kid Pix, or any word processing program using large font.

Try This!

If you have a sewing machine available, make books for children's writing by layering several sheets of paper together with a cardstock cover and sewing down the edge or on a middle fold. The cardstock can be covered with colorful wrapping paper or wallpaper to add interest. Parents might be happy to make these books for the classroom. Books can also be made in a variety of shapes, such as circles, squares, or a shape associated with your topic of study. Animal books are easy to make by folding construction paper in half and cutting out a half circle across from the fold to form the legs and body of the animal. Children could add faces and tails. Paper plates offer possibilities for book covers as well and could also be used as an animal face or body. Provide a variety of materials children can use for adding features, such as wiggly eyes, pipe cleaners, or plastic forks to form feet or antlers.

Writing Throughout the Day

Children need many opportunities to write in order to increase their skills and understanding of the writing process. These experiences can happen in large and small groups, as well as individually. Model writing for a purpose throughout the day. Take advantage of situations that arise when you may need to write something down, such as a note to remind yourself of something or a message to the custodian. Write your note so children can listen as you think out loud about what letters and words you are using.

An inviting writing area stocked with book-making supplies also promotes children's writing. Add words with pictures that correspond with the topic you are studying for children to use in their writing. Provide writing materials at many of the interest areas around the room, such as sign-making materials in the block area, and notepads in the dramatic play area for children to use in making grocery lists or writing notes to each other. Consider setting up an office in the dramatic play area with the children and discuss what supplies might be needed. Families may be able to donate recycled paper, telephones, briefcases, sticky notes, in- and out-boxes, and other items. Children could make their own business cards, as well as a variety of other written materials.

Try This!

Ask families to send in empty cereal boxes to use for making mailboxes for each of the children. Cut off the top portion of the box, and invite children to cover their boxes with construction paper and decorate it to look like a house. Place the mailboxes on a chalk ledge or a low shelf where children can access them easily. Encourage children to write letters and put them in each other's mailbox houses. They can also write letters to family members and store them in their mailboxes to take home. This can be done in conjunction with setting up a Post Office in the dramatic play area and remain out for the rest of the year to encourage children's writing.

Author Studies

Point out the authors in books you read to the class. Consider focusing on one author at a time, and encourage children to find similarities in the books an author has written. Several authors have videos available on the Internet describing their work, which will deepen children's understanding of the work of an author. Construct a bulletin board highlighting one author at a time. Invite children to create illustrations using similar techniques as the featured author and add them to the bulletin board.

Talk about what an author does and help children realize that they can be authors too. After each of them has had the opportunity to make one or more published books, invite families to an authors tea where children can read their books. Offer refreshments and share other work that children have been doing.

Try This!

Bring large rolls of paper outside for children to use in writing *BIG* stories like teacher Sarah Skatvold. Bring out a variety of markers, crayons, and other art materials children can use to make their stories come to life on the paper. Children can work individually, in pairs, small groups, or as a class. Depending on their skills, they could dictate stories to an adult or older child in the school or do their own writing.

DISCOVERING MORE ABOUT LEARNING NEW LANGUAGES

Kindergarten is an ideal time for children to begin learning a new language. Recent research on the brain suggests that hearing the sounds of language help children form connections in the brain that make language learning possible. Without these connections in place, learning a new language will be more difficult when students are older. Children can learn beginning words in new languages by listening to and singing songs in these languages. They can listen to audio books in both English and another language at the listening area. There are also tapes and CDs especially designed to help children learn a new language, such as *Speak Spanish with Dora and Diego.*

Teach children simple greetings in other languages and use these greetings as children come in from recess or other times during the day. Learn number words and provide opportunities for students to count in meaningful situations using these new words. Doing an Internet search will result in finding sites that provide help in learning new languages, including pictures and audio pronunciations. Invite family or community members who speak a language other than English to come in and teach some simple conversational words. Practice these words frequently to help children remember them. Label items around the room in both English and another language, such as Spanish. Read bilingual books and then include them in the library area where children can explore them further. There are a number of bilingual and alphabet books in a variety of languages children will enjoy.

SUPPORTING CHILDREN LEARNING ENGLISH AS A NEW LANGUAGE

Many of the strategies that help all of our children develop language and literacy skills will also help children who are learning English as a new language. Using big books that allow children to see the words as you read and point to them is especially helpful. Reading bilingual books that include their home language can help children make connections with what they already know in their native language. Provide interesting audio books in the Listening Area that will help children become more familiar with the English language. Encourage children to read to each other in pairs, making sure that children learning English are paired with children who have good language and literacy skills. Sing enjoyable songs repeatedly, using a song chart and pointing to the words as you read. Invite family and community members who speak children's home languages to come in and take dictation from the children in their native language and then translate the words into English under the dictated words. Send home simple bilingual books that families can read together. Let families know you value their language and culture and encourage them to continue to include their native language at home.

WORKING WITH CHILDREN'S INDIVIDUAL NEEDS

Differentiating instruction is necessary to meet children's individual needs (Strickland & Ayers, 2007). Research demonstrates that it is important to provide additional instruction and intervention as soon as we notice that a child is having difficulty. Knowing where individual children are in their literacy development helps us to meet them where they are and provides the support they need to gain additional skills and strategies. While children are busy working and playing in interest areas, we can work with individuals and small groups. Use multiple copies of simple leveled texts to read with children in small groups. Books that are at children's current skill levels improve fluency and self-confidence, while those that are just beyond their current levels should provide just the right amount of challenge. Provide individualized support with individual writing conferences. For some children, this may begin with writing a single letter they hear at the beginning of a word, while other children may advance to writing simple stories. Learning a new language by listening to tapes or CDs and reading more advanced books are beneficial activities for children who are ready for additional challenges.

Summary

Language and literacy can be woven into every fiber of the kindergarten day. It is important to keep in mind key goals that will help children become successful readers and writers. Children can meet these goals in developmentally appropriate ways through engaging studies and experiences, including many opportunities for reading and writing for authentic purposes. It is important for teachers to frequently assess children's literacy development and provide support that will continually scaffold them to reach higher levels. When children experience enthusiasm, joy, and success in their early efforts to read and write, they are more interested in continuing their efforts, and look forward to participating in the community of readers and writers.

7

Motivating Mathematics

Children enter kindergarten with a wealth of knowledge about mathematics, which serves as a foundation for more formal learning in school. Our task is to discover their levels of competence and provide rich experiences for them to build on this foundation and move forward in their learning. We want to help children not only learn mathematics, but enjoy it, understand it, and be able to use it confidently in their day-to-day lives. As children strive to make sense of mathematics in their world, we can encourage them to talk about their thinking, supporting their efforts as they build communication skills as well as mathematical understanding.

What Research and the Experts Tell Us

In their joint position statement *Early Childhood Mathematics* (2002), the National Council of Teachers of Mathematics (NCTM) and the National Association for the Education of Young Children (NAEYC) made several recommendations for providing high quality mathematics learning for young children:

- Encourage children's natural interest in mathematics and their disposition to use it as they try to make sense of their world.
- Support learning by connecting to children's prior experiences and knowledge and taking into consideration family, linguistic, and cultural backgrounds.
- Build on children's problem solving and reasoning processes and integrate learning with other subject areas.
- Allow time and materials for children to engage in play to explore materials and expand on mathematical ideas.
- Incorporate appropriate experiences and teaching strategies and continually assess children's mathematical knowledge and skills.

It is important for teachers to help children develop confidence and enjoyment in doing mathematics. A positive approach toward learning mathematics enhances children's interest in exploring possibilities in problem solving and reasoning. When children are engaged in play, they have a wealth of opportunities for learning mathematics and practicing the skills that support mathematical understanding. Play provides opportunities to revisit concepts in an enjoyable context. As teachers, we can support their play by introducing math manipulatives, being there to ask provocative questions, and giving children ample time to explore and discover mathematical concepts through play.

DESIGNING THE ENVIRONMENT TO PROMOTE MATHEMATICAL THINKING

Through thoughtful planning, we can provide an atmosphere that will encourage kindergarteners to learn skills, become mathematical thinkers, and meet standards. This can begin by setting up an inviting math area filled with engaging materials that beckon them to explore and investigate. Adding a number line displaying the numerals one to 20 can help children begin connecting numbers to their daily activities and help them see numbers in sequence. The number line could be on the wall, the floor, or both to help children physically experience numbers increasing and decreasing as they line up objects or stand on the line themselves. As the year progresses and children gain confidence working with numbers, increase the numbers to 25. In the last quarter of the year, tape a picture of a quarter under the numeral 25; add pictures of a dime, nickel, and penny under their corresponding numerals as well.

Include an assortment of objects to practice counting skills, such as counting bears, colorful cubes, dominoes, and keys, as well as natural items. Unit blocks help children to learn about shapes and the relationship of one shape to another. Children love to measure with both nonstandard and standard units of measure. A balance scale, clock, calendar, measuring cups, and child-safe thermometers are tools that can bring meaning to mathematics for children. Give children opportunities to use quality software and Web sites, such as the National Council of Teachers of Mathematics' Illuminations at http://illuminations.nctm.org. Providing a variety of the right tools can put children on track for becoming confident, young mathematicians!

Try This!

Consider storing math activities in unusual containers in the math area to engage students and add interest. Try putting materials into lunch boxes, backpacks, doctor kits, large purses, sturdy gift bags, or wicker baskets. One bag could hold strands of beads that have been cut into lengths of one bead, two beads, and so on up to 10 or 20. Children can put these in ascending or descending order or use them for measuring and counting.

Include math tools in many areas of the classroom. Plastic inchworms or links in the science area allows students to measure and record the growth of plants or classroom pets. Children can use play dough to form numbers, shapes, or make patterns. The block area itself is a welcoming place for children to learn math, especially geometry. Provide a variety of shapes for building, including cylinders, cones, and cubes. Sand and water tables offer wonderful opportunities for working with volume and weight and offer real-life applications of terms such as more, less, and the same. The outdoor environment offers rich possibilities for learning math as well. Kindergarteners can look for shapes in the environment, check the outside temperature, go for number walks with clipboards to search for numbers on signs, count trees, and measure the widths of sidewalks.

ADDRESSING STANDARDS AND DEVELOPING MATHEMATICAL CONCEPTS THROUGH ENGAGING STUDIES AND EXPERIENCES

By intentionally planning engaging experiences, children can be learning math throughout the day, beginning with taking attendance, reviewing the calendar, and graphing the weather. This is an excellent time to introduce a problem of the day, such as *How many carrots will our guinea pig eat in three days if she eats two carrots each day?* Children can be thinking about how to solve the problem and then discuss and show their solutions later in the day.

Set aside additional time each day to focus on math concepts. After working on a concept or problem together, children can work in pairs or small groups doing hands-on activities with manipulatives or at centers set up around the room to reinforce the concept you are investigating. For example, after talking about standard units of measure and measuring objects together, children could work at centers where they can practice measuring a variety objects, using rulers and meter sticks.

In addition to meeting content standards, children need to acquire *process standards* to support their problem solving, reasoning, and communication skills. Long-term studies or investigations can help children develop these skills. A project on tools can provide opportunities to use a variety of tools to think through and solve problems. If new construction is going on in the neighborhood, children might enjoy pursuing that as a topic of investigation, opening up new possibilities for making connections, representing new understandings with a variety of media, and communicating this new knowledge with others.

The National Council of Teachers of Mathematics (NCTM) has developed content standards in the areas of

- Number and operations
- Algebra
- Geometry
- Measurement
- Data analysis and probability

In addition, NCTM has also developed curriculum focal points and connections that can help guide our work. Number and operations, geometry, and measurement are focal point areas for key learning in kindergarten. These areas of study are most important for children this age and form the foundation for later mathematical concepts. Connections in these three areas should also be made to studies in data analysis and algebra. Information on these focal points can be found at http://www.nctm.org/focalpoints.

Discovering More About Number and Operations

The first NCTM curriculum focal point for kindergarten is number and operations and describes the knowledge, skills, and concepts we should help children in kindergarten understand. NCTM describes this focal point as:

Number and Operations: Representing, Comparing, and Ordering Whole Numbers and Joining and Separating Sets

Children use numbers, including written numerals, to represent quantities and to solve quantitative problems, such as counting objects in a set, creating a set with a given number of objects, comparing and ordering sets or numerals by using both cardinal and ordinal meanings, and modeling simple joining and separating situations with objects. They choose, combine, and apply effective strategies for answering quantitative questions, including quickly recognizing the number in a small set, counting and producing sets of given sizes, counting the number in combined sets, and counting backward.

Reprinted with permission from *Curriculum Focal Points for Prekindergarten through Grade 8 Mathematics: A Quest for Coherence*, copyright 2006 by the National Council of Teachers of Mathematics. All rights reserved.

Our goal is to help children become familiar with what numbers are, understand their relationships, and recognize how they help us in our daily lives. Children will need many experiences to be able to make sense of numbers. Use both cardinal and ordinal numbers in meaningful situations: *First, we will plant the seeds; our second step will be to water them; and the third step will be to set them in the sunlight.*

Give children opportunities to count all year long. At the beginning of the year, hang a roll of cash register tape or other long strip of paper horizontally across the wall, writing one number each day with the children to indicate the number of days of school. Designate a special color for days ending in *five* and another color for days ending in *zero* to help children see the patterns in number sequences. Students can practice counting the days by fives and tens.

The 100th day of school can be an exciting event to look forward to and a day filled with mathematical learning! As the year progresses, count the days leading up to the 100th day, highlighting days 25, 50, and 75 with special activities and making special note to count down the last 10 days. Plan engaging activities for the 100th day that will deepen children's knowledge of numbers. Help students count out 100 building blocks and then encourage them to work with a partner to build using only those 100 blocks. Children could use 100 snap cubes to build a wall five cubes high or stretch 100 links to form a shape. *Miss Bindergarten Gets Ready for the 100th Day of Kindergarten* is a favorite book to read at this time of year and suggests additional activities to celebrate the day.

Ten frames are useful for helping children learn to visualize numbers from one to 10. A ten frame is a rectangular shape that includes two horizontal rows of five sections each. By giving children many experiences using ten frames they can begin to *subitize* (or know how many objects there are just by looking and not having to count each one) that there are five or 10 items. With even more practice, they will begin to recognize other number combinations as well, leading to understanding basic math facts to 10. For example, they will begin to recognize that if the top row is filled and one more object is on the bottom, they have $5 + 1 = 6$.

Try This!

Try making ten frames from a variety of materials:

- An ice cube tray with 10 compartments
- A foil pan taped off in sections of two rows of five with colored tape
- Colorful placemats or carpet samples with lines added to make two rows of five
- Ten napkin rings, canning jar rings, or shower curtain rings forming two rows in the lid of a shoebox

Make ten frames to correspond with the topic you are studying by using 10 small cups with topical decorations or stickers.

Find an attractive plastic container to use as an *estimation jar*. Attach a label that will explain to families that students can fill the jar with 20 or less of an item when it is their turn. Send the jar home with a different child each night and ask that it be returned the next day with items that allow students to practice their estimating and counting skills. You could begin by asking for 10 items or less and gradually increase the number throughout the year. Instead of sending the jar home, students could also take turns filling the jar with items from the classroom. Later in the year, create an *estimation museum*. Ask students to place items in containers and invite another class to visit and estimate how many objects are in each container.

Developing communication skills is vitally important for kindergarten children. During math time, offer opportunities for children to use words to tell how they solved a problem. Begin the year by working on simple problems using the names of children in the class, such as *Jamal has two dinosaurs and Dominique has three dinosaurs. How many do they have all together?* Allow children a few moments to process on their own what the problem is asking and a strategy to solve it. Then encourage group discussion and suggest they use manipulatives, dramatize the problem or make simple illustrations to represent their reasoning. Children should come to realize that there is more than one way to solve a problem.

Young mathematicians need to be able to use concrete objects to demonstrate their mathematical thinking. Provide a variety of manipulatives for students to use and allow them to work in small groups to solve the problem. Assist them by asking thought-provoking questions as they work. Ask students to verbally share with others how they solved the problem. As their skills increase, help children record their thought processes by drawing pictures, writing words, or eventually writing a number sentence to show how they solved the problem.

Try This!

Ask questions that will cultivate children's mathematical thinking. Consider hanging a list of questions in your room, such as

- What are we trying to find out?
- What do we already know?
- What were you thinking to get that answer?
- Is there another way to solve the problem?
- Can you prove your answer?

Help children boost their literacy skills and build connections between mathematics and literacy by reading interesting counting books, such as *12 Ways to Get to 11*. Read the book for enjoyment the first day. On the second day, read it again and have children join you in counting each of the items on the pages. Later, set up a center where children can make their own pages for a class book, following a similar pattern to that used in the book. For example, after reading *10 Black Dots*, children could pull a number out of a hat and make a picture containing that number of dots. The center could include sticky dots, stickers, nontoxic bingo markers, small pom-poms, and other art supplies shaped like dots. Gather the children's completed work to make a class book. Read the book together frequently over the next several weeks and then let children take turns bringing the book home.

As children progress in their understanding of numbers and counting, make sure that children not only can count a group of objects accurately but also that they are able to tell us that the last number they count tells how many are in the group. Ask children to count a group of objects; when they finish, ask them to tell you how many there are. If they need to recount, you know they need support to master this task. Give them many opportunities to count throughout the day, and model with activities such as counting the children each day and then asking, *So how many are here today?*

Discovering More About Geometry

The second NCTM curriculum focal point for kindergarten is geometry.

Geometry: Describing shapes and space

Children interpret the physical world with geometric ideas (e.g., shape, orientation, spatial relations) and describe it with corresponding vocabulary. They identify, name, and describe a variety of shapes, such as squares, triangles, circles, rectangles, (regular) hexagons, and (isosceles) trapezoids presented in a variety of ways (e.g., with different sizes or orientations), as well as such three-dimensional shapes as spheres, cubes, and cylinders. They use basic shapes and spatial reasoning to model objects in their environment and to construct more complex shapes.

Children can be learning geometry throughout the day, especially as they spend time constructing in the block area. Playing with blocks helps children develop spatial awareness, which helps with physical development and fine motor skills, as well as concepts needed for social studies and map reading. If we join in their play, ask questions, and converse with children, we can extend their learning. Encourage children to talk about the physical attributes of the three-dimensional objects they are using, as well as the similarities and differences. Students will be building math, language, and social skills as they interact with you and their classmates. Add books, such as *Alphabet Under Construction*, to integrate even more literacy and problem-solving opportunities.

Try This!

Make your own blocks with boxes and wallpaper. Use sturdy boxes (like those that Capri Sun® individual servings are packaged in) and wrap the boxes in wallpaper just as you would wrap a gift. Fasten the edges securely. Connect several boxes together with strong packing tape and wrap with the wallpaper to form a chair or table. Children can help you brainstorm ways to arrange the boxes to put the furniture together.

Provide many examples of shapes, oriented in a variety of positions. When discussing shapes, first ask children what they notice about the shape. How many sides does it have? Are there angles? Listen for the words they use and introduce the mathematical terms they need to learn. For example, if a child is looking at a triangle and says, "*It has three pointy things,*" you could say, "*Yes, we call those angles and there are three of them.*" Show shapes from many different points of view. Give children toothpicks or drinking straws in different lengths to build triangles. Challenge children to make triangles in different sizes. Continue to ask what children notice about them and then begin to help the children make generalizations. Triangles all have three angles and three sides, but they can be many different sizes and orientations. Record children's understandings about triangles on a chart that they can refer to over time. Then begin work with shapes having four sides. This will help children think about and learn the attributes of different shapes.

Give children the opportunity to grow in their geometric thinking by providing pattern blocks, along with the outline of simple shapes to fill in. Once children can fill in very simple forms, gradually increase the difficulty so that children are combining shapes to fill in the forms. Challenge children to combine shapes to build bigger and more complicated shapes.

Try This!

Put together a *birthday bag* to reinforce geometry concepts. Fill a festive birthday gift bag with play dough, cookie cutters of various shapes, birthday candles, and a book that includes interesting shapes. The book *The Secret Birthday Message* by Eric Carle includes a map featuring various geometric shapes that lead to a birthday gift; children could make their own map and message using shapes. Allow students to enjoy playing with the contents in the gift bag with several friends on their birthday. If there is a child in your room whose family does not wish to have them celebrate birthdays, save this activity for another year.

Discovering More About Measurement

The final NCTM focal point for kindergarten is measurement.

Measurement: Ordering objects by measurable attributes

Children use measurable attributes, such as length or weight, to solve problems by comparing and ordering objects. They compare the lengths of two objects both directly (by comparing them with each other) and indirectly (by comparing both with a third object), and they order several objects according to length.

Reprinted with permission from *Curriculum Focal Points for Prekindergarten through Grade 8 Mathematics: A Quest for Coherence*, copyright 2006 by the National Council of Teachers of Mathematics. All rights reserved.

Measurement includes linear measurement, area, capacity, weight, temperature, and time. Measurement is an important part of children's lives and something they take great joy in doing. Kindergarteners are interested in how tall they are, how far they can throw a ball, which pumpkin weighs more, and how many days until a special event. Provide children with many opportunities to apply measurement skills throughout the year to help them meet this standard. Begin by asking them to compare two different objects using words such as taller, heavier, or shorter. Once these comparisons are understood, begin to offer nonstandard units of measurement.

Young children need many experiences with nonstandard measurement in order to build their own understanding of why we need standardized measuring tools. Ask children to measure the length of the tables in the classroom using a variety of nonstandard items, such as paper clips or shoes. Help children record their measurements and ask what they notice about the number recorded for the length of objects when different units of measure are used. *Why do we have different numbers for the length of the same object?*

Once children have discovered some of the disadvantages of nonstandard units of measure, provide them with many opportunities to measure with rulers, yardsticks, and metersticks. Children delight in these experiences and can learn a great deal as they measure and record their findings both indoors and outside.

Give children many opportunities to weigh a variety of objects using a balance scale. Occasionally, ask them to predict which object will be heavier or lighter. Use the scale to make comparisons and encourage children to record their findings with illustrations and words.

Discovering More About
Data Analysis (Making Sense of Data)

NCTM recommends that we should help children make connections to data analysis.

Data Analysis

Children sort objects and use one or more attributes to solve problems. For example, they might sort solids that roll easily from those that do not. Or they might collect data and use counting to answer such questions as, "What is our favorite snack?" They re-sort objects by using new attributes (e.g., after sorting solids according to which ones roll, they might re-sort the solids according to which ones stack easily).

Provide occasions for children to work with data on a regular basis. Offer activities for them to classify, organize, represent, and use information to ask and answer questions through play and exploration. As a first step in making sense of data, give children many experiences sorting and classifying. Provide a variety of containers to use in their sorting, such as colored bowls, cupcake tins, or baskets. Encourage children to sort by a variety of attributes, such as color, size, and shape. Make use of meal and snack times to learn more about classification by talking about characteristics such as types and colors of food.

Help children gather data by posing questions for their classmates to answer, such as hair color or favorite book. Place pads of paper where children can access them easily; children would be motivated to use a magnetic pad of paper posted on a file cabinet for gathering data. With adult support, students could write their survey questions and ask classmates to respond by signing their names or placing tally marks by their answers. After collecting the data, students will need to know how to organize and make sense of their information. Suggest making a graph with the results of the survey so the data can be seen clearly. Make graphs of every day experiences and as a complement to your topics of study. For example, if you're studying transportation, graph what vehicle they would most like to ride in.

Try This!

Make a graphing mat from an inexpensive, white shower curtain, plastic tablecloth, or pattern cutting board. Make graph lines with colored tape or permanent marker. Having sections about six inches square will allow room for placing actual items on the graph, including children's shoes or colored blocks. Temporary graphing mats can be made from paper or cardboard to post in the room, allowing children to learn from them for an extended period of time. Set a goal to make at least one graph each week with your children.

Discovering More About Algebra

NCTM recommends that kindergarten teachers should also help children make connections to algebra.

Algebra (Including Patterns)

Children identify, duplicate, and extend simple number patterns and sequential and growing patterns (e.g., patterns made with shapes) as preparation for creating rules that describe relationships.

The main focus of algebra in the kindergarten classroom is on patterns and relationships, which lays the foundation for future study. Children should be given many experiences in sorting and classifying interesting materials according to first one, and then several attributes. Simple patterning activities can be introduced using these physical materials and should increase in difficulty as children gain confidence. Model making simple patterns such as *red, blue, red, blue,* and ask children to extend the pattern. Invite the children to get involved physically by making people patterns, such as *girl, boy, girl, boy.* Later, have the children make patterns by having one child *stand,* and the next child *sit.* They can also perform action patterns, such as *clap, snap, clap, snap.* Help children develop more abstract thinking by beginning to describe their patterns as *A-B-A-B* when making these simple patterns. When they demonstrate this understanding, progress to a more advanced pattern, such as *A-A-B-A-A-B,* saying this aloud as they perform actions such as *hop, hop, point; hop, hop, point.*

Try This!

Ask parents to bring spare buttons to contribute to a button box. Encourage children to sort the buttons in as many different ways as they can and use the buttons to make patterns. Read books, including *The Button Box,* and books with repetitive patterns.

Children will enjoy incorporating patterns into their artwork. Challenge them to make a pattern frame around a special drawing or design a placemat with rubberstamps repeating a pattern. Offer colorful beads and cords that children can use to create patterns they can wear.

Opportunities for Authentic Assessment

Use the NCTM curriculum focal points to make a checklist of mathematical knowledge, skills, and concepts you want to help children acquire. Ask children to individually demonstrate their understandings of items on the list during day-to-day experiences with hands-on materials, such as counting out cups needed for snack or measuring the bean seedling they planted. Observe children counting items to assess their counting skills. Do they have a strategy for counting accurately, such as moving an item aside after it has been counted? Ask children to demonstrate their thinking about how to solve problems using manipulatives and drawings. *How many brushes will we need if we want two brushes in each of these paint cups?* Watch as children make patterns in the art area or sort objects in the math area and ask them to describe their process.

SUPPORTING CHILDREN LEARNING ENGLISH AS A NEW LANGUAGE

Kindergarten children who are learning the English language will require special consideration when learning mathematics. Be sure to offer a wide variety of manipulatives for children to practice their math skills. Count numbers in English as well as the languages spoken by your children and sing counting songs in English and other languages. Use simple words to describe what you are doing as you make patterns, graphs, sort, and do other math activities. Scaffold their learning by intentionally teaching mathematics vocabulary and speaking in clear, simple terms. Whenever possible, model what to do, rather than just telling, to help children better understand. Partner children with other children who speak English well and can help them learn math terminology.

WORKING WITH CHILDREN'S INDIVIDUAL NEEDS

Mathematics is an area where children who have difficulty learning may be able to find a connection to real-life situations. As they learn more about numbers they will be able to use this knowledge in authentic situations as they count toys to share or measure ingredients for a special snack. If math is meaningful and enjoyable, there is more reason to want to learn it! Encourage students to use manipulatives when counting and provide a nonslip surface mat to help manage the pieces if needed. Make sure the block area is physically accessible to all children. Gluing sandpaper, fabric, or other textures to blocks or other shapes will add to the sensory experience. Use puff paint to make raised domino dots for students who are visually impaired. Teach children basic sign language to help them communicate their mathematical understanding.

As you get to know your children, you may find that some have a special talent for doing mathematics. Serve their needs by adjusting the difficulty of math problems to their level. Encourage them to think of new ways to solve a problem and to write in a journal reflecting on their learning. Help them to create math games using dice or number cards. Encourage them to do surveys of their own and collect data, organize it, and communicate their findings. Provide opportunities for children to play quality games on the computer that increase in difficulty to meet each child's level.

Summary

The National Council of Teachers of Mathematics has developed curriculum focal points for kindergarten that are of primary importance for learning at this age. Kindergarten focal points are in the areas of number and operations, geometry, and measurement and will build the foundation for later mathematical concepts. Connections should also be made to studies in the areas of data analysis and algebra. To enhance learning, we can provide an environment with a variety of manipulatives to actively engage children in understanding mathematical concepts. Math can be incorporated into daily experiences and combined with literature to enhance literacy skills as well. Math concepts will develop as children play in interest areas, construct with blocks, explore volume in the sand and water table, make patterns, and use problem-solving skills on the computer. Our goal should be to help children develop positive attitudes toward mathematics, see a connection between math and their everyday lives and realize that learning math is something they are able to do and can be fun!

8

Celebrating Creativity Through the Arts

The arts provide young children with the opportunity to make meaning of their world and experience joy as they grow in their creativity and self expression. Kindergarteners are able to express their thoughts and feelings through art long before they are able to communicate through written words. Empower children to use the arts to learn new ways to solve problems, to see the world in a new way, and make connections to cultures around the world. By offering experiences in the arts, we can help children value and respect their own work, as well as that of others, and learn to express themselves imaginatively through a variety of media.

What Research and the Experts Tell Us

Jalongo and Isenberg (2006) describe the importance of the creative arts by affirming, "Creative thought and expression is more like the root system of the tree of learning than the small leaves and twigs, for without creative thought, learning in any of the subject areas is stunted and cannot flourish" (p. 123). Their recommendations for kindergarten teachers include helping children develop: an understanding of creativity and their own creative thought processes, respect for various ways of thinking, strategies to develop ideas and work on them intensely, and an ability to assess their own work. They recommend that teachers reject ready-made craft projects, and give children genuine choices and time to carry out their ideas. According to *Developmentally Appropriate Practice in Early Childhood Programs* (Copple & Bredekamp, 2009), teachers should offer open-ended art experiences and integrate the arts into other areas of the curriculum. They should not provide models that children are expected to copy. Instead they should encourage children to explore a variety of media and movement, and encourage them to expand on their ideas.

DESIGNING THE ENVIRONMENT TO PROMOTE CREATIVITY THROUGH THE ARTS

Setting up an art area allows children the freedom to work independently with a supply of art materials that boost creativity. Display art materials attractively on low shelves in containers that invite exploration. Allow time for children to focus on the process of art as they work to investigate different techniques and explore new ways of using various media. Encourage creativity in the visual arts by including a wide assortment of paper in a variety of colors and sizes. Provide crayons, markers, drawing pencils, colored pencils, pastels, chalk, and other drawing instruments to allow children to choose just the right tool for their art. Even recycled materials and other *beautiful stuff* (Topal & Gandini, 1999), such as buttons, wood scraps, yarn, ribbon, and fabric can be used to design collages and other artwork. Include an art easel for two or more children to use at the same time to encourage communication and sharing of ideas. The easel can be available for daily use to add a new dimension and workspace for young artists. Be sure to allow adequate space and time for children to get deeply involved in their art and be able to continue to work on it for extended periods of time.

A dramatic play area with engaging props and materials is a natural place for children to meet standards in the arts. Establishing a music area in your classroom will also support children's growth in reaching standards. Include instruments such as drums, xylophones, bells, triangles, and rhythm sticks as well as rain sticks, maracas and other multicultural instruments. Provide tapes and CDs of favorite music. Adding scarves or ribbons to the area will encourage children to dance and move to the music.

The schools in Reggio Emilia, Italy, have become known around the world for the art their children create. In Reggio, children are viewed as strong, capable, and full of potential. Teachers provide instruction in art techniques and skills to help children represent their learning in the context of long-term projects. Children are encouraged to use many different ways to express themselves, including drawing, painting, singing, dancing, and construction, which they refer to as *the hundred languages of children*. The environment is designed to support children with an array of materials they can use to represent their understandings and provide provocation to help them advance in their work and their thinking (Wurm, 2005). Reggio schools strive to help children learn to care for and respect each other, the materials, and their environment. They believe that children, teachers, and parents "should be surrounded by spaces that will enhance our lives, support our growth, and hold us in respectful ways" (Cadwell, 2008, p. 374).

ADDRESSING STANDARDS IN THE ARTS THROUGH ENGAGING STUDIES AND EXPERIENCES

National Standards for Arts Education in kindergarten through 12th grade were developed by the Consortium of National Arts Education Associations and include the areas

- Visual Arts
- Music

- Dance
- Theater

They provide a guide and resource that describe what children should know and be able to do in the arts. A complete list of these standards may be found at http://artsedge.kennedy-center.org.

The arts offer many opportunities for long-term investigations. Kindergarten children love playing all kinds of musical instruments and may enjoy doing a study of music or sounds. They might also enjoy exploring topics related to artists and illustrators along with the works of art they have created.

Discovering More About the Visual Arts

The visual arts include a wide range of art including painting, drawing, sculpting, and designing. Provide basic instruction in techniques, such as how to draw a face and body, and how to use different media. Let children explore these processes in the art area with a wide variety of open-ended materials. Learning new techniques will help children express their ideas, and provide them with new vocabulary, tools, and media to express their thoughts. The best art activities will require little teacher preparation, but will require teachers to offer support as children experiment with the creative process.

Play dough and clay are wonderful materials to help kindergarten children develop their creativity and artistic skills. Making play dough with a small group of children can be a fun art activity, but can also integrate mathematics and literacy. Writing out the recipe on a large sheet of paper and pointing to the words as children add ingredients helps them use literacy and numbers in a meaningful way. They can take turns counting out and adding ingredients while you talk about interesting words such as *ingredients* and *batter*. After the ingredients have been added, pass the bowl around for children to take turns stirring and counting to 10 in various languages before passing the bowl onto the next child. Science enters the scene when children are asked to predict what will happen to the mixture when it is poured into the skillet and heated.

Recipe for Play Dough

2 cups flour

1 cup salt

2 cups water

4 teaspoons cream of tartar

4 tablespoons of oil

Food coloring or washable water color

With the children, add ingredients and mix together. Mixture will be a thin batter.

(Continued)

(Continued)

Additional ingredients can be used for a more sensory experience, such as cinnamon, vanilla, powdered drink mix, or dry, flavored gelatin mix. An adult can pour the mixture into a skillet and cook on medium heat, stirring constantly until it thickens. Allow to cool. Children enjoy kneading the play dough while it is still warm, but not hot to the touch.

It's fun to make a fresh batch each month, allowing children to choose the color. Later in the year, try doubling or tripling the recipe and talk with the children about how they could do that using their regular recipe. Children could also make their own individual batches of play dough by making a fraction of the recipe.

Setting out a large tray with play dough in the art area is an easy activity to prepare and can be varied by occasionally adding different props, such as alphabet cookie cutters, safety scissors, or craft sticks. Encourage children to make letters, words, shapes, and numbers with the play dough. Provide a cupcake pan and birthday candles, and encourage students to have fun exploring math concepts as they play with these materials.

Consider giving children opportunities to take photographs (Good, 2009). Ask parents to bring disposable cameras as part of their school supplies or simply share a classroom camera. Children can learn to view the world *with the eyes of a photographer.* They can take photographs, study them, and then try to recreate the image with paint, crayons, play dough, or other media. This could become one aspect of a long-term study on buildings and architecture as children photograph various styles of buildings or a special study of nature with photographs of plants, flowers, or trees. Ask children to think of other things to photograph and allow them to continue taking pictures as long as their interest and imagination are sustained.

Think about other possibilities for taking art outside for inspiration. Bring the painting easels outdoors and hang paper on a fence or the building. Provide the colors of nature and allow children to paint the world as they see it. Collect items from nature to make collages, including seeds, pebbles, and leaves. Help children press flowers and leaves by placing them between the pages of an old phone book or newspaper weighted down for several days. Children can make beautiful note cards or artwork by placing the dried flowers on cardstock and covering them with sheets of clear contact paper. Collect scraps of lumber from a building supply store and encourage children to sand the wood, glue pieces together to make constructions, and then paint their creations.

Study the works of various artists, discuss their techniques, and encourage children to try similar techniques in their artwork. In your discussions, include vocabulary such as line, color, shape, and composition. Include artists such as Vincent Van Gogh, Claude Monet, and Georgia O'Keefe. Children may also enjoy learning about Piet Mondrian who was born in Holland and spent time as a school teacher before devoting his life to art. Share examples of his artwork from books or the Internet and ask children to think about how he might have created his paintings. Children could try their hand at creating similar works. Let children know how artists sign their work and encourage them to do the same.

Include rolls of masking tape in the art area for children to use in their work. Demonstrate how they can cut strips of tape and attach them to a sheet of paper in interesting patterns. Children can then paint the sheet with diluted tempera paint or spatter paint with a toothbrush. After the paint is dry, they can remove the tape and delight in the positive/negative creation that is left behind. Add tapes of varying widths, sizes, and color that children can continue to explore in the area.

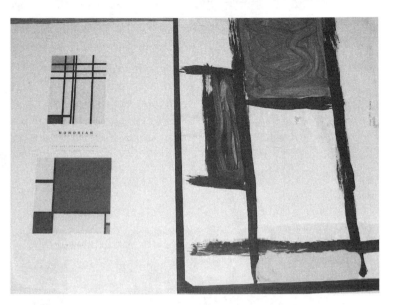

Integrating the arts with other subjects helps children meet standards in the arts, as well as other areas of the curriculum. Connect art and literacy by reading quality children's literature and studying the process that illustrators use in creating their books. Look at an illustrator's work and encourage children to try using similar techniques in their artwork. Authors and illustrators such as Eric Carle, Lois Ehlert, Jan Brett, and Leo Lionni offer exceptional books for thoughtful study and investigation.

Art and science go hand in hand when we offer experiences in recycling and taking care of the earth. In a long-term study of paper, children could help you make recycled paper and marvel that they can actually make new paper from paper they have already used. Throughout the year, encourage children to save scraps of colored construction paper. When you have a good supply, they can sort the paper by color and begin tearing it into

small pieces. Soak the paper scraps overnight with enough water to completely cover the paper. An adult can then use an electric blender to grind the paper mixture into pulp. Pour the pulp into cups and invite children to pour spoonfuls of the pulp into cookie cutter shapes or jar-ring lids placed on an old window screen or other screen placed over a container to catch the water as it drips from the pulp. A simple screen can be made by stretching nylon hose over a hanger. Press the pulp with a sponge to remove excess water and allow it to dry for several days. The recycled paper makes lovely decorations for greeting cards or beautiful framed pictures.

Try This!

Make homemade crayons! Invite children to sort old crayons, peel off the paper, and fill metal soup cans half full of similarly colored crayons. An adult can put the cans in a heated water bath in a skillet to melt the crayons. Keep children safely away from the hot wax. Stir the crayons occasionally with wooden craft sticks. When melted, pour the liquid crayons into candy molds and allow them to cool and harden. Large molds with solid shapes work best, such as teddy bear or ice cream cone shapes. Rainbow block crayons can be made by pouring layers of melted wax into small plastic cups one colored layer at a time. Allow each layer to cool almost completely before adding the next layer of color.

Integrate life science with art by planting marigold flower seeds in a colorful cup as a gift for family members. Children can decorate the cup and add a miniature watercolor masterpiece they have painted on a small square sheet of paper. Mat the paintings on slightly larger pieces of construction paper and attach the paintings to colorful craft sticks placed in the cups.

Let children know you respect and value their artwork and help them gain confidence by displaying it in the classroom. Simple construction paper frames or clear acrylic frames work well to showcase children's artwork. Consider having an art show and inviting family members, other classes, or members of the community to view children's artwork in an open house showing.

Try This!

Suggest that parents begin a three-ring binder to hold and display their children's artwork.

Discovering More About Music

Music adds beauty to our lives and can be a source of joy and comfort to children. What better way to start the day than with a beautiful, meaningful song in their hearts? Research has found that music can enhance the connections in the brain and lead to better outcomes in reading and math. Take every opportunity to incorporate music throughout the day. Children will meet music standards as they take pleasure in singing alone and with others and enjoy listening to music.

Singing songs at the beginning of the day helps build a community of learners. Find a special good-morning song to sing with children to welcome them to a new day of friends, fun, and familiar routines. One of the benefits of singing is that a song can be repeated often. If the songs are written on chart paper, children will make literacy connections as you point to the words and ask them to find repetitive phrases. Supply instruments for children to use to accompany the songs and keep a steady beat to the rhythm. Encourage children to play musical instruments and march with the beat like a marching band.

Choose songs that have a good message that will remain with children throughout the day. Songs such as "Inch by Inch," "The More We Get Together," "Thanks a Lot," and "To Everyone in All the World" teach valuable lessons for life.

Try This!

Make songbooks with favorite songs in large print. Include songs in one or more other languages as well. Ask family members to translate a song into children's home languages for inclusion if possible. Enjoy using the songbooks frequently in class and send home at the end of the year for children to continue literacy learning as they share songs with their family.

National Standards for Arts Education suggest that children understand the relationships between music and other areas. Music can be integrated with literacy as children sing rhyming songs, such as "This Old Man" or "Down by the Bay," which will build phonemic awareness. Challenge students to substitute new words for the rhyming words in a song. While reading books, such as *Chicka Chicka Boom Boom,* children could play instruments when the words for the title of the book are repeated throughout the story.

Songs can help children learn days of the week, months of the year, color words, counting, and other concepts when the words are put to music. Sing "Five Little Ducks" and write out the math problems with numerals and pictures as the song introduces them:

5 little ducks minus 1 little duck = 4 little ducks

Invite children to use rubber ducks, cubes, or other manipulatives to model the problem as well. Later in the year, do this same activity with songs, such as "There Were 10 in the Bed."

Children can blend music and math in other ways as well. As they gain expertise in creating patterns, ask them to set the patterns to music. If they have created an *A-B-B-C, A-B-B-C* pattern on paper, encourage them to enjoy using three different musical instruments to play a tune that represents the pattern.

Talk with children about the instruments they hear in music; the *Nutcracker Suite* is a fascinating piece of music to analyze. Introduce music of different cultures and genres to help children learn to recognize and appreciate various types of music.

Try This!

Make egg shakers to add to your musical instrument collection. Provide colorful plastic eggs for children to decorate with markers, paint pens, glitter, sequins, or other craft materials. They can use salt, bird seed, sand, or other materials to fill the eggs, experimenting with varying amounts to produce different sounds. Tape or glue the eggs shut and encourage children to have fun shaking to the beat of the music.

Discovering More About Dance/Movement

Dance or movement experiences offer many benefits for kindergarten children. Through dance, they are able to express inner feelings, learn about other cultures, experience different types of music, and make connections between dance or movement and healthy living. Before undertaking studies in dance it is important to know and understand the families of children you are working with. Be sensitive to families' cultures and beliefs. If there are families that do not wish for their children to participate in dance, there are many good movement activities you can do instead.

Play a variety of music and encourage children to dance or move to the beat. Include music that is fast, as well as slow, and ask children to compare and contrast the two through their movements. Encourage children to talk about the feelings they experience when they hear different pieces of music and to express those feelings through their movement. Provide props for children to use in their movement, including scarves, pom-poms, or strips of lightweight fabric.

Try This!

Make dancing streamers for children to use as they move to music. Begin with a paper plate. Help children attach crepe-paper streamers or ribbons in a variety of colors, and use their creativity to decorate them.

Play music from a variety of cultures and teach simple dances from those cultures, such as an Irish jig or Mexican hat dance. Teach partner skills, such as repeating or doing a mirror image of another child's movements. Invite families to teach simple songs, dances, and movements from their cultures.

Provide opportunities for children to tell stories through dance and movement, including a sequence with a beginning, middle, and end. After reading a book, encourage children to create a dance to celebrate the story or retell a favorite story through dance and movement. Children can use movement to reenact science events, including the metamorphosis of a butterfly or frog, an approaching storm, or an exploding volcano.

Emphasize the importance of physical movement for healthy living and enjoyment. Dance and move throughout the day to keep children active and engaged. Include dance and movement outside on a regular basis.

Discovering More About Theater

The dramatic play area can be the center of rich learning in the kindergarten classroom. Children can be reaching theater standards as well as standards in all curriculum areas as they work with stimulating materials and become deeply involved in their play. As they interact with each other in this area, children are able to practice real-life situations as they make-believe and take on new roles to become the baker, postmaster, astronaut, or farmer.

Converting the dramatic play area to compliment your topic of study will expand children's learning and vocabulary. They will become more engaged in the area if they feel some ownership in creating the setting. Once your study is complete, materials can be stored in *drama boxes* or *prop boxes* for use in future years with a ready supply of theme-related objects for play. Be sure to add reading and writing materials along with other props, such as

- Post office box with posters, writing materials, envelopes, stickers, and stamps
- Restaurant box with menus, signs, ordering pads, play money, and cash register
- Veterinary office box with stuffed animals, doll bed, pillows, and doctor's kit

Talk with children about services that are provided in each unique setting. Encourage children to demonstrate qualities such as helpfulness, neighborliness, kindness, and teamwork as they play together in the area.

Opportunities for Authentic Assessment

Encourage children to represent what they have learned in other areas of the curriculum through the arts. Ask children to use a variety of media to draw pictures, create songs, dances, and puppet shows to demonstrate their understandings.

SUPPORTING CHILDREN LEARNING ENGLISH AS A NEW LANGUAGE

Children learning English as a new language can learn new ways to express themselves through visual arts, music, drama, and dance. Help them learn the vocabulary associated with the arts and label supplies in the art area with words and pictures to facilitate efforts in this area. Talk about the art process and use expressive language to build vocabulary. Sing songs in both English and their native languages and use props to increase understanding. Use labels and signs with pictures in the dramatic play area and let children help in making and posting them. Encourage conversations between children learning English and those already proficient in the language.

WORKING WITH CHILDREN'S INDIVIDUAL NEEDS

All children benefit from good teaching practices in the arts that allow them to focus on the process of art and encourage creativity and expression. Some children may require special adaptations to be able to fully participate. This may include large handles on paint brushes for easier grasping or magnifying glasses for close observation. Easels may need to be lowered and can be made from wood or cardboard to fit on a table. Hearing devices may be used to fully appreciate the sounds of music. Turning up the bass on CD players can help children feel the beat. Children who are unable to sing can participate by playing a musical instrument. Make certain that all children have physical access to the dramatic play, art, and music and movement areas and feel they belong to the community of artists in the room. Children who have special talents in any of these areas should be encouraged to pursue avenues that develop their potential. Provide materials, time, and support to promote each child's growth in the arts.

Summary

National Standards for Arts Education were developed by the Consortium of National Arts Education Associations and include the areas of visual arts, music, theater, and dance. Children can meet standards in the arts when we offer them opportunities to explore a wide variety of materials, tools, and processes and introduce various techniques for creative expression. The arts should be included throughout the day and can enhance learning in all other areas of the curriculum. Children should be encouraged to develop their ideas and be given time and materials to become deeply engaged in their art. Teachers should provide experiences for children to learn about and appreciate a variety of art from their own neighborhoods, as well as from cultures around the world.

9

Promoting Healthy Physical and Social-Emotional Development

indergarten is an ideal place for children to form positive habits and attitudes that will lead to a lifelong healthy lifestyle. Positive attitudes toward themselves and others, as well as positive approaches to learning, will build a foundation that will support learning and social interactions. Developmentally appropriate activities and experiences and a nurturing environment fosters these attitudes. Establishing healthy habits toward eating and exercising can help prevent childhood obesity, which is increasing at alarming rates and has become a nationwide concern.

The National Association for Sport and Physical Education (NASPE) has developed standards as well as documents outlining appropriate practices for physical activity and movement programs. According to Sanders (2006), there are a number of benchmarks children should be able to do by the end of the kindergarten year, including

- Walk and run using mature form
- Demonstrate clear contrasts between slow and fast movement while traveling
- Identify fundamental movement patterns, such as *skip* and *strike*
- Establish a beginning movement vocabulary (such as *personal space, high/low levels, fast/slow speed, light/heavy weights, balance,* and *twist*)
- Identify and use a variety of relationships with objects (such as *over/under, behind, alongside, through*)
- Toss a ball and catch it before it bounces twice
- Kick a stationary ball using a smooth continuous running step
- Recognize that physical activity is good for personal well-being
- Share space and equipment with others
- Recognize the joy of shared play

- Interact positively with classmates regardless of personal differences (such as race, gender, or ability)
- Associate positive feelings with participation in physical activity
- Try new movements and skills (p. 132)

Opportunities for Authentic Assessment

Make a checklist with these benchmarks and assess children as they play outside and in activities and experiences you have designed.

DESIGNING THE ENVIRONMENT TO PROMOTE HEALTHY PHYSICAL DEVELOPMENT

Both the indoor and outdoor environment can contribute to children's physical development and invite them to move, play, learn, and grow. Create spaces that encourage children to actively participate and provide just the right amount of challenge, both physically and mentally. Make use of the outdoors when possible for children to play with a variety of balls, plastic racquets, and other equipment. Children love activities involving large parachutes and can learn both social and physical skills in this play. Set up an obstacle course occasionally both outside and indoors and describe children's actions as they go over, under, through, behind, and alongside objects in the course.

Consider creating an activity station with a variety of materials that change over time, including bean bags and scarves. The activity station could be inside, outdoors, or both. Set up a low balance beam in the station or invite children to construct one with long blocks that they can use as they walk from one area to another. Provide written directions and pictures that describe a special exercise to do each week in the station.

Create interest areas that promote fine motor development by including materials that both boys and girls will find appealing, such as Legos®, puzzles, pegboards, beads, lacing cards, a variety of art and writing tools, and scissors that make decorative cuts. The dramatic play area provides possibilities for children to use fine motor skills as they dress dolls, dial phones, and use plastic utensils. Converting the area to a clothing shop will give them additional practice in buttoning, snapping, and zipping clothes.

Try This!

Kindergarten children love to sew! Create a little sewing nook where several children can sew with an assortment of colorful yarn and blunt plastic needles with large eyes. Provide fabric that the needles can pass through easily, such as burlap. Parents and fabric stores may be able to donate fabric scraps and yarn. Allow children to be creative in their designs. Decorate the area with textile art or pictures of star quilts and tapestries.

ADDRESSING STANDARDS AND FOSTERING PHYSICAL DEVELOPMENT THROUGH ENGAGING STUDIES AND EXPERIENCES

Children need the guidance of a caring adult who will provide encouragement, instruction, and play-based opportunities to practice in order to optimally develop physical skills (Sanders, 2006). Consider the possibility of establishing a routine of taking a daily walk with your children, either in the neighborhood, around the playground, or even inside the building. This is a wonderful way to inject some movement into the day and model this healthy habit.

Healthy physical development can be integrated into all areas of the curriculum and incorporated naturally into studies. Children can walk to field sites and build fine motor skills as they write and create art connected to their topic. In a study of the community or community helpers, children could practice several motor skills by "delivering" newspapers. Enlist children's assistance in decorating a delivery box and writing "newspaper delivery" on it. Children can take on the role of a newspaper delivery person by rolling up newspaper, placing rubber bands around them or stuffing into plastic newspaper bags, and then practice throwing them into the delivery box (Sanders, 2002).

Try preparing healthy snacks with the children weekly or monthly. Many families would be happy to contribute ingredients. Children are more willing to try healthy foods when they are involved in preparing it. Spatulatta Cooking 4 Kids Web site (http://www.spatulatta.com) has easy recipes children can join in preparing. The site includes videos demonstrating preparation of a variety of cultural dishes. Write out recipes for snacks that are easy to prepare, using simple words and pictures in step-by-step sequence.

Incorporate even more literacy by reading books, such as *Eating the Alphabet* or *Gregory the Terrible Eater*. Assist children in writing healthy menus on the computer that they can use in the dramatic play area. Include clip art that gives picture clues of the written words.

Propose noncompetitive games that keep all children actively involved rather than those that eliminate individuals who then remain inactive. Build in opportunities for brief exercise and movement during group times to help children stay alert and focused. Suggest stretching while waiting in line. Occasionally, skip or march when traveling from one place to another. Music adds enjoyment to exercise for children as well as adults. Play a selection of invigorating music while you stretch, exercise, and move. Inviting families to share their cultural dances and enjoying dances together, such as the *Hokey Pokey*, the *Twist*, or a jig can help build a feeling of community in the classroom.

As children's fine motor skills mature, their handwriting also develops. Give children many opportunities to write for authentic purposes, including signing in and writing notes to family and friends. Specific handwriting instruction and practice can be done with small groups during interest area time. Avoid working on handwriting skills during writers workshop when the focus should remain on creating meaning and conveying a message through their writing.

Activities that promote physical development can be woven throughout the entire day. After reading a book such as *From Head to Toe* by Eric Carle, in which children imitate animals' actions, set up a center where children can make their own version of the book. Provide paper with the words from the book

I am a _____

and I can _____.

At the lower left corner of the paper include, "Can you do it?" with "I can do it" at the lower right corner.

Children can fill in the names of their favorite animals (or create animals) and actions their animals can do. Children could make one page at the center each day for a week to make their own book or contribute one page to a class book. Afterward, children can read their pages and perform the actions. This activity could be done even without the Eric Carle book and is a fun way to promote physical activity, as well as an attitude of being able to accomplish things on their own, a key factor of social and emotional development. The remainder of this chapter will discuss additional ideas for fostering children's social and emotional development, which was one of the major reasons for establishing the first kindergartens.

DESIGNING THE ENVIRONMENT TO PROMOTE POSITIVE APPROACHES TO LEARNING AND SOCIAL-EMOTIONAL DEVELOPMENT

Thoughtfully planning the design of the room can promote positive approaches to learning and social-emotional development. Engaging interest areas with interesting hands-on materials will spark curiosity, eagerness, invention, and imagination. Science and math areas that invite children to investigate will advance problem solving and reflection. The dramatic play area provides abundant opportunities to practice social skills and develop friendships as children cooperate to negotiate roles, settings, and play themes. Each interest area offers potential for growth in social skills, as children help each other at the computer, collaborate on building in the block area, and have fun investigating science concepts together in the sand and water tables. Ensuring that there are enough materials for children to comfortably share will make interactions in these areas more positive. Children's social and emotional development thrives in a predictable, stable, calm atmosphere where they feel welcomed and significant.

NURTURING POSITIVE APPROACHES TO LEARNING AND SOCIAL-EMOTIONAL DEVELOPMENT THROUGH ENGAGING STUDIES AND EXPERIENCES

What Research and the Experts Tell Us

Developing positive approaches toward learning in the early years makes it possible for children to take advantage of learning opportunities as they continue in their education. Being enthusiastic contributes to children's interest, joy, and motivation to pursue learning. Enthusiasm, initiative, persistence, inventiveness, curiosity, problem-solving ability, and other positive learning behaviors are cultivated over time with the help of caring adults who encourage children's engagement in a supportive, motivating environment (Hyson, 2008).

Fostering Positive Approaches to Learning

Studies that provoke children's interest and curiosity are ideal for building positive approaches to learning. As children pursue answers to their questions and learn additional information about topics that interest them, they become more inquisitive and aspire to find out even more. Visiting interesting places and listening to visitors share information and intriguing materials on project topics can sustain motivation.

Read stories about fascinating people, places, and events. Design interest areas with materials that beckon children to come and explore. Arranging interest-area time so that children are able to make choices and stay deeply involved in an activity promotes initiative and persistence. Set up investigations that children can perform successfully on their own in the science area, along with magnifiers, magnets, and other captivating equipment. Offer engaging materials in the math area that children will be eager to use for measuring, sorting, and making patterns. Stock the writing and art areas with paper in a variety of shapes and sizes, along with many different types of writing instruments and art supplies. Add interesting textures to paint with sand, salt, coffee grounds, and glitter. Leave materials out for extended periods of time to support children's persistence, but rotate materials and add new items to promote their invention and imagination (Jacobs & Crowley, 2007).

Try This!

Set up an *invention station* or *creation station* in your room where children can invent their own creations. Change the materials occasionally to keep their creative juices flowing. Start with wood scraps, sandpaper, glue, and paint. Later, children could make new creations with boxes of varying sizes and shapes, buttons, pipe cleaners, glue, and tape. Look around your room for possible supplies, and ask families to contribute *beautiful stuff*, such as fabric scraps, pom-poms, seeds, colored paper clips, and a variety of paper and cardboard. Add books that may serve as inspiration with pictures of inventions and beautiful sculptures. Include pictures of inventors and their inventions, making sure to include both women and men from diverse ethnic backgrounds, such as George Washington Carver, Alexander Graham Bell, and Henry Ford. You could also include Ann Moore, inventor of the *Snugli*, who got the idea for the baby carrier when she was in the Peace Corps and observed mothers in Africa carrying their babies.

To promote children's problem solving and reflection, encourage them to view mistakes as opportunities to learn. Suggest that they think about alternative ways to remedy the situation. Teach them the steps in the problem-solving process and post them in the room.

Problem-Solving Steps

1. What is the problem?

2. What can we do? *Brainstorm possible solutions*

3. What shall we try? *Choose a solution*

4. Let's give it a try. *Try out the solution*

5. Did it work? *Evaluate*

6. If not, what else shall we try? *Start the steps over*

Fostering Healthy Social and Emotional Development

One of the first and most significant strategies we can use to support children's social and emotional development is to form relationships with each of our children and their families. When children know that we care, honor, and respect them individually, their sense of self-worth increases. They are also more likely to care about what we have to say and notice the example we set. A positive climate where children feel accepted as individuals with their own strengths, interests, and challenges contributes to building a healthy self-concept for all children. Letting children know we recognize their efforts, academically, physically, and socially is an effective way to scaffold the development of their positive self-concept. Hearing continuous criticism and negative remarks can have the opposite effect. Display children's art and writing at their eye level and talk with them about progress they are making. Share books about diverse children, families, and cultures, such as *Something Beautiful, Families,* and *Families Are Different.* Let children know you value them as special and unique individuals. Help children see the beauty and worth of differences as well as support their growth in the appreciation and acceptance of each other's diversity.

Try This!

Add an "about the author" page to books that individual children have written. Ask children to dictate information about themselves as you type or write down their words. This is a wonderful way to foster self-esteem while boosting literacy skills!

As our relationships strengthen through rich conversations and spending time together, children come to trust us and eventually learn to trust others. They can learn from our example how to treat others with care and compassion. Once relationships are formed, there are many ways that teachers can scaffold kindergarten children's social and emotional development, including helping children build pro-social behavior and attitudes, social interaction skills, and self-regulation skills (Tomlinson, 2009).

Forming friendships is important to children's social and emotional development. Teachers need to intentionally teach pro-social skills that help children establish these friendships. Discuss qualities that make a good friend and make a list with the children to post in the room, along with pictures portraying the qualities. Give children specific words they can use when starting up a friendship, including simple greetings and questions to help in getting to know each other. *Hi, how are you? What do you like to play? Would you like to do that now?* This can be done in large and small groups with children role-playing and offering suggestions. Assist children individually on the playground, in the dramatic play area, and anytime you notice a teachable moment. Occasionally, join in children's play to help foster budding friendships.

According to Bronson (2006), "It is also important that adults attribute pro-social qualities to the child. When children are frequently told that they are 'helpful,' 'generous,' or 'kind,' they internalize these attributions and try to exhibit them in the future. Positive attributions also help children understand that motivation and control of social behavior come from inside themselves, and that they are responsible for their actions" (p. 53).

Try This!

When you address children, think about addressing them as *friends: Good morning, Friends; Time to go outside, Friends; Ask your friends if they can help you.* This strengthens their images of themselves as people who can befriend other children, and who others, including you, would enjoy having as friends.

Plan activities that assist children in getting to know and respect each other. Make graphs of children's eye and hair color, gender, as well as favorite books, activities, and foods to help them get to know each other. Add characters from favorite books for additional diversity or to support a child who might be the only one with a certain characteristic. Provide opportunities for students to work in pairs and small groups to get to know each other better.

Discuss the emotions of characters in books, as well as those that children are experiencing. Support children in recognizing their own emotions, and then recognizing and being sensitive to the feelings of others. This will assist them in developing empathy and begin to recognize that others may have different perspectives. Encourage children to help each other and work toward developing a sense of community and cooperation in the classroom. Provide opportunities for students to share job responsibilities in the classroom. Comment when you notice children sharing and being kind to one another.

Suggest occasions for extending kindness to others in the school, including writing thank you notes to the principal, janitor, guidance counselor, assistants, and parent volunteers. Write class thank you notes frequently to model an attitude of gratitude, good manners, and social skills.

Try This!

Make thank you notes by folding a large sheet of paper in half and drawing circles around the border of the card, corresponding with the number of children in the class. When you want to send a thank you to someone, write the message together and then ask children to draw their faces in the circles with multicultural crayons or markers and sign their names next to their faces. Faces can be drawn inside the card as well.

Kindergarten teacher Lisa Carroll asks each child to draw a self-portrait and sign it. She uses a photocopier to reduce the size of each picture, and arranges these small images around the border of a 12- × 18-inch piece of paper. This creates a unique thank you note that can be photocopied for use throughout the year and sent with personalized messages for each occasion.

Assist children in developing empathy and concern beyond the walls of the school. Make cards for the elderly or children in the hospital. Be on the lookout for situations that fit your children and setting, which could include singing at a nearby nursing home, planting trees, helping with cleanup and recycling efforts, or collecting food, clothing, or books for children in need.

Children with good self-regulation skills are able to control their emotions and behavior. These skills can be taught over time in an environment where children feel safe and have a sense of belonging and community. Teaching steps involved in problem solving can help children think of alternatives to frustration or anger they may feel when difficulties arise. Use class meetings as time to work on solving problems together.

Good teaching and planning help us provide effective behavior management. Providing a variety of interest areas and large blocks of time when children can freely move from one area to another may decrease behavior problems because children are not expected to quietly sit still for extended periods of time. Kindergartens that have many interesting activity choices and developmentally appropriate expectations, experience less difficulty with behavior management.

There are children who come to kindergarten with challenging behaviors. Although it may take time and effort, developing positive relationships with these children is especially important. Finding the cause of the challenging behavior is a necessary step. Once we know the cause of a behavior, it becomes possible to find ways to channel it in more positive directions. If children are having difficulty sitting quietly, consider limiting the amount of time for whole group activities. Work with smaller groups while others are happily engaged in interest areas where they can be exploring, moving, and talking as they learn. Make certain that there is always something for children to be engaged in when they finish their current activity. Eliminate times that children have nothing to do but wait; make the time more productive with songs, poems, and rhyming games.

Be patient with yourself and the students, realizing that small steps can eventually lead to the desired goal. Notice children's attempts at good behaviors and provide positive feedback, letting them know how much you appreciate their efforts. You may need to do this frequently at first but less often over time as children's self-regulation increases.

Preventing problems is easier than trying to overcome them. Think about your activities, schedule, and expectations, looking for any adjustments you might make to prevent future concerns. Researchers have outlined protective factors that help children, even when their lives are disruptive. By helping children develop these factors, they become more *resilient* and have less need to exhibit challenging behaviors. These factors include *social competence, problem-solving skills, autonomy and self esteem,* and *sense of purpose and future* (Kaiser & Rasminsky, 2003). The Devereux Institute has a set of music CDs, titled *Songs of Resilience,* that speak of *initiative, self-control,* and *attachment,* key ingredients for protective factors and building social and emotional development. As children play in interest areas, they can be listening to enjoyable songs that help them with impulse control, learning to plan, thinking about the consequences of potential actions, being good friends, and having confidence in their abilities.

Involve parents as partners in building children's resilience and working on social and emotional development at home. Send home books they can read with their children, such as *Franklin Helps Out* and *Making Friends.* Compose newsletters letting them know what skills you are working on in school and suggesting activities they can do at home. One note could mention the *Songs of Resilience* CDs that parents might wish to purchase as music to play as children fall asleep at night. The family calendar in Resources at the back of this book contains daily suggestions families can do at home with their children, including involving children in simple helpful tasks, reading and talking together, and helping them appreciate the wonder of the world around them.

Try This!

Collaborate with families to promote resilience factors and literacy by creating a book, titled *Acts of Kindergarten Kindness,* to send home with children. Find an appealing stuffed animal that will fit into an available backpack and introduce it to the children, suggesting that the young animal wants to come home with each of them to learn how to be kind. Add multiple pages to the book that read

I love my family at the top and

I can be kind by _____ at the bottom of each page, leaving the middle as blank space for pictures.

Inside the cover of the book, tape a letter explaining to families that when children bring home the backpack, they can draw a picture of how they demonstrated kindness at home. Then they could dictate a sentence about their act of kindness that a family member could write under the picture. Include washable art materials. Once the backpack has been to each child's home, send it home again with pages that read

I love my family.

I can help by _____ .

Include different art materials and suggest that children help in writing about their kind act.

SUPPORTING CHILDREN LEARNING ENGLISH AS A NEW LANGUAGE

Develop a rapport with each child. Let children know that you value each of them individually. Demonstrate respect for children's home languages and cultures by getting to know a few words in each child's language. Check with families to be sure you are pronouncing children's names correctly. Enlist the help of family members to make simple bilingual books in both English and the child's home language. Incorporate sight words that children need to be learning and use a predictable pattern such as, *I can . . .* or *I see. . . .* Invite family members in to prepare healthy recipes from their home cultures with the children. Snack and meal time can be used as opportunities to have conversations and practice using new words in a meaningful context. Sing the "Hokey Pokey" and "Head, Shoulders, Knees, and Toes;" and play Simon Says, emphasizing the words to the body parts as you point to them. Check frequently during activities to make sure children understand.

WORKING WITH CHILDREN'S INDIVIDUAL NEEDS

Provide many opportunities for children to practice skills and build strength and stamina. Adapt activities so all children can participate as fully as possible, develop self-confidence, and feel like capable members of the class. Break tasks into small, achievable steps that allow children to meet with success each step along the way and acknowledge their attempts. Use modeling and pictures to help children grasp concepts. Supply adaptive equipment and materials if needed, such as modified keyboards, switches, standers, and adapted seating to allow children to take part in activities. Place rubber mats or other nonslip surfaces under puzzles or other materials to keep them from slipping. Make transitions easier for children by letting them know how much time they have before they will need to stop their activity. Providing five-, three-, and one-minute alerts can help children who have difficulty with transitions. Designate special songs for cleanup or other challenging times of the day to help children know they'll need to end one activity and begin another. The Center on the Social and Emotional Foundations for Early Learning at http://www.vanderbilt.edu/csefel/ has a wealth of information and materials that can help with children who have social and emotional challenges.

Discover each child's individual strengths and needs. Begin wherever children are and help them progress. For children who are more advanced, provide activities that help to stretch them intellectually, rather than simply giving them more work. Foster their positive approaches to learning by suggesting topics they might like to investigate further and providing access to books and other resources. Encourage children to help each other. This is beneficial to children at all points of the educational continuum; teaching a concept or skill to someone else is one of the best ways to practice and learn it at a deeper level.

Summary

It is important for children to form positive habits and attitudes early in life in order to build the foundation for future healthy living. Developmentally appropriate activities in a nurturing environment can help to foster these attitudes. Daily exercise and opportunities to play, both inside and outdoors, as well as eating healthy snacks and meals helps children reach standards. A caring adult who intentionally plans experiences and provides encouragement is necessary for children's development in both the physical and social domains. By forming relationships, teachers can get to know children, their strengths and needs, and scaffold their development. Engaging studies, activities, and investigations can help children develop positive approaches to learning, which will enable them to make the most of future learning. Demonstrating our care, honor, and respect for children as we present engaging educational and social opportunities helps to increase their sense of self-worth and pro-social skills. Providing experiences that help children gain protective factors of social competence, problem-solving skills, autonomy, self-esteem, and sense of purpose assists them in becoming resilient individuals. They will then be better able to regulate their behavior and emotions and benefit more from their time in the classroom.

10

Connecting the Dots

Reaching Standards and Beyond

A developmentally appropriate kindergarten can become the corner-stone for building a lifelong love of learning. To build this strong foundation, teachers need to set challenging but achievable goals for their children and continually make decisions about the best ways to help students achieve them. In a developmentally appropriate kindergarten, teachers intentionally plan experiences based on their knowledge of how children develop and learn, as well as their understanding of each of their individual children and their social and cultural contexts (Copple & Bredekamp, 2009). In addition to knowing the children, teachers need to be knowledgeable about the content children are expected to know in each area of the curriculum and methods that will help their individual children learn this content (Heroman & Copple, 2006). Standards outlined by states and national professional organizations can serve to outline that content and guide our work with children.

There are many engaging strategies teachers can use to support children in meeting standards, including both child- and adult-guided experiences. Designing an engaging environment with interest areas and centers that offer a variety of motivating materials and activities allows children to learn new skills and practice those they have already acquired. Kindergarten schedules need to allow time for children to become engaged in interest areas, as well as time for large and small group activities, and time to play and make choices both inside and outdoors.

Research has validated the importance of play, including free play, to children's social, emotional, cognitive, and language development (Wenner, 2009). When children have rich opportunities for play,

> they can more easily solve problems, communicate their ideas with more fluency, and show more empathy toward their friends. They can even practice leadership skills when they put forth new play

ideas. In enumerating the tremendous learning that can take place in play, we can see that the lessons of play extend far beyond childhood. Being able to think imaginatively, resolve conflict with grace, trade ideas with others, and be compassionate are the building blocks for human relationships (Heidemann & Hewitt, 2010, p. 218).

Investigations or studies also provide opportunities for children to learn as they explore concepts in depth. Studies focusing on science and social studies topics support children in meeting standards in these subjects as well as in all areas of the curriculum.

Every moment of the kindergarten day offers possibilities for joyful learning, through reading books, writing stories, creating art, as well as investigating science and math. Even routines and transitions present occasions for discovery and meaningful conversations, songs, poems, and rhyming games.

KINDERGARTEN FOR ALL CHILDREN

Every child deserves the opportunity to have a quality kindergarten experience. The National Association of Early Childhood Specialists in State Departments of Education (2000) recommends that all children be "enrolled in kindergarten based on their legal right to enter" (p. 7). They suggest that families not be counseled to keep their children from entering kindergarten and that the wishes of the family be respected. They also recommend that children be welcomed as they are and not set apart into extra-year programs before or after the kindergarten year.

Children who are old enough but are deemed *unready* may be those who would most benefit from a quality kindergarten experience. Neuroscience research confirms that the first five years of life are critical to brain development. Children need quality, nurturing environments to form the connections in the brain that will become the basis for all future learning. Keeping children out of kindergarten may deprive them of making the best use of this opportune time when the brain is most receptive. Rather than delaying entry until they are judged to be *ready*, we need to be ready for them with ready schools and ready communities who will support their development and learning.

It is important to continually assess children throughout the year to understand their current knowledge and skill levels, meet them wherever they are, and scaffold their progress. This should be done in authentic and meaningful ways, including the use of observations, checklists, and portfolios that demonstrate children's growth through samples of their work. These assessments should be shared with families who can join us in using them to set future learning goals. Forming reciprocal relationships with families cultivates partnerships that serve to support children's development. This collaboration will have lasting benefits for children and families long after the kindergarten year.

THE LENGTH OF THE KINDERGARTEN DAY

The quality of the teaching and the quality of the curriculum are of utmost importance to children's learning in kindergarten. Being able to experience this quality teaching and curriculum for a full day increases learning opportunities and benefits for kindergarten children. Research has shown that students in full-day programs make higher academic gains than children in half-day or every-other-day kindergarten programs (Elicker, 2000). Additional benefits of full-day programs include more individualized time with students and small groups, more time for assessment and instruction, and the potential to get to know students and families better (Nelson, 2000; Porch, 2002). Full-day programs also provide the opportunity for children to spend a longer portion of the day in a higher-quality program than might otherwise be affordable for some families (Vecchiotti, 2001). "Full-day kindergarten programs should be available—and affordable—to *all* children," according to Kagan and Kauerz (2006, p. 163). They do suggest, however, that families have options in terms of length of day and setting when possible.

SUPPORTING THE TRANSITION TO FIRST GRADE

Regardless of the length of the day, thoughtfully planning a smooth transition to first grade supports children in continuing on a successful path of learning. This can begin early in the kindergarten year by providing opportunities for children to interact with first grade students, including viewing special projects and events in each other's rooms, reading and writing with each other, and joining in community service activities.

Families can be invited to a special event to meet the first grade teachers and learn more about the curriculum and activities in the upcoming year. This information could be shared through a slide show with photographs taken throughout the year. Children's work could also be on display. A joint picnic, ice cream social, or activity night for kindergarten and first grade children, families, and teachers allows them to get acquainted and begin establishing relationships. Providing suggestions of enjoyable activities families can do together over the summer will help children continue learning and be eager to start a new year. A calendar with simple ideas to share with families through the transition to first grade can be found in the Resources at the back of this book.

REACHING BEYOND THE STANDARDS

While meeting standards is a significant facet of our work with children, it is not the only one. Our vision includes children becoming lifelong learners who are happy, enjoy positive relationships with family and friends, and develop into concerned, participating members of society. To make this dream come true, we need to continually evaluate our programs and seek ways to make our classrooms and schools places that lead to this goal.

In their book, *Teaching Goodness*, Goodman and Balamore (2003) describe a kindergarten classroom that focuses on helping children develop respect, responsibility, honesty, peace, and other characteristics that allow them to be good citizens of their classroom and community. Usha Balamore, who was the teacher in this classroom, carried out yearlong themes that captured and held children's interest and permitted her to concentrate on these characteristics. The themes took a variety of twists and turns that led them through all areas of the curriculum. The topic of heroes involved reading biographies, investigating shared qualities of heroes, learning about local heroes in the community, and discussing how they could be heroes through community service activities. The study led to research about the body, which included science, health, and art as they visited an art museum and made their own sculptures.

Another yearlong theme revolved around a mama bear searching for a good classroom for her baby bear where he could learn respect and responsibility. Wanting to provide a good environment for the baby bear, children explored concepts such as patience, respect, responsibility, and kindness to the earth. The class wrote a book about how they could demonstrate respect in various settings, and wrote individual respect and responsibility stories about characters who demonstrated these qualities. Children received encouraging notes about their efforts throughout the year from the mama bear. In the context of daily activities, they were encouraged to think about the feelings of others and to make good choices because they were the right things to do, rather than for external rewards. Students learned to think about the needs of others, as well as meeting their own needs.

This kindergarten classroom was described as "a romance, a *falling in love with goodness*" (Goodman & Balamore, 2003, p. 34). As we make our weekly plans with engaging literacy, math, and science activities, we can also think about experiences that encourage our students to *fall in love with goodness.* Teach children how to resolve conflicts and solve problems. Talk about how to be a peacemaker at home and at school. Foster an atmosphere where children care about each other and become a community of learners who help and nurture each other.

Try This!

Introduce an attractively decorated *kindness box* containing paper, pencil, and a list with children's names and pictures, following the model of teacher Usha Balamore. When children notice someone exhibiting kindness, ask them to write down the name of the person, along with a picture or written description of the kindness they observed. Once a week, open the box and celebrate the kind deeds. Make it a point to notice and write about children's kindness yourself, including a few different children each week so that each child receives recognition and encouragement.

Forming meaningful relationships with children makes it much more possible to reach goals both academically and socially. We can strengthen our relationships and increase the quality of our interactions by creating a positive climate, showing regard for students' perspectives, and being sensitive to their needs. Students will feel more connected to us and each other and feel safe taking on new challenges, trusting that we will be there to support them. Engaging in rich back-and-forth conversations and feedback on a regular basis with each child not only enhances our relationships but fosters language, social, and academic skills (Pianta, LaParo, & Hamre, 2008).

When children develop positive attitudes toward learning and feel confident in their abilities, they increase their motivation to continue learning throughout life. A good foundation for these positive attitudes is a deep sense of wonder about the world, including themselves and those around them. Rachel Carson (1965) noted that, "If a child is to keep alive his inborn sense of wonder he needs the companionship of at least one adult who can share it, rediscovering with him the joy, excitement, and mystery of the world we live in" (p. 54). Those who work with kindergarten children have the great privilege and responsibility to sustain this awe and intentionally plan experiences that will help them develop and preserve

- Amazement and appreciation for living things and the diversity of life
- Love of nature and a desire to care for the earth
- Interest in becoming contributing members of their family, class, and community
- Lifelong love of reading and an ability to communicate their thoughts through writing
- Appreciation for the arts and expressing themselves creatively
- Healthy, active lifestyles
- Positive approaches to learning
- Strong sense of self-worth as kind, loving, capable people who are able to solve problems
- Profound sense of wonder and true joy in learning

Resources

Children's Books

Aliki. (1990). *My hands*. New York: HarperCollins.

Aliki. (2000). *All by myself*. New York: HarperCollins.

Amery, H. (2003). *The Usborne first thousand words in Spanish*. Tulsa, OK: EDC Publishing.

Base, G. (1986). *Anamalia*. New York: Harry N. Abrams.

Binch, C., & Hoffman, M. (1991). *Amazing grace*. New York: Penguin Young Readers Group.

Bourgeois, P. (2000). *Franklin helps out*. New York: Scholastic.

Brett, J. (1985). *Annie and the wild animals*. New York: Houghton Mifflin.

Bridwell, N. (1999). *Clifford's first school day*. New York: Scholastic.

Brown, M. W. (1957). *Good night moon*. New York: Harper & Row.

Brown, M. W. (1995). *Buenas noches luna*. New York: HarperCollins.

Carle, E. (1986). *The secret birthday message*. New York: HarperCollins.

Carle, E. (1997). *From head to toe*. New York: HarperCollins.

Cheltenham Elementary School Kindergarten. (2003). *We are all alike . . . We are all different*. New York: Scholastic.

Cohen, M. (1989). *Will I have a friend?* New York: Aladdin Books.

Dennis, Y., & Hirschfelder, A. (2003). *Children of Native America today*. Watertown, MA: Charlesbridge.

Ehlert, L. (1990). *Fish eyes:A book you can count on*. New York: Harcourt Brace.

Ehlert, L. (1996). *Eating the alphabet*. San Diego, CA: Harcourt Brace.

Ehlert, L. (1996). *Feathers for lunch*. San Diego, CA: Harcourt Brace.

Ehlert, L. (1998). *Nuts to you*. San Diego, CA: Harcourt Brace.

Emberly, R. (2000). My opposites/Mis opuestos. Boston: Little Brown. Boston: Little Brown.

Engelbreit, M. (1994). *Over the river and through the woods*. Kansas City, MO: Andrew McMeel.

Fleming, D. (1992). *Count!* New York: Henry Holt.

Flemming, D. (2006). *Alphabet under construction*. New York: Henry Holt.

Freeman, D. (2002). *Corduroy goes to school*. New York: Penguin Putnam.

Hamanaka, S. (1994). *All the colors of the earth*. New York: Harper Trophy.

Harper, C. (2008). *Charley Harper's ABCs*. Los Angeles, CA: Ammo Books.

Hoban, T. (1974). *Circles, triangles, and squares*. New York: Simon & Schuster.

Kilgras, H. (1997). *What will I do if I can't tie my shoe?* New York: Scholastic.

Lioni, L. (1975). *A color of his own*. New York: Dragonfly Books.

Martin, B., & Carle, E. (2007). *Baby bear, baby bear, what do you see?* New York: Henry Holt.

Martin, B., & Archambault, J. (1989). *Chicka chicka boom boom*. New York: Simon & Schuster Children's Publishing.

Morris, A. *Families*. (2000). New York: HarperCollins.

Pearle, I. (2008). A *child's day: An alphabet of play*. San Diego, CA: Harcourt Children's Books.

Pellegrini, N. (1991). *Families are different*. New York: Scholastic.

Penn, A. (1993). *The kissing hand*. New York: Scholastic.

Parr, T. (2001). *It's okay to be different*. New York: Little, Brown, Hatchette Book Group.

Pimsluer Staff. (2008). *Speak Spanish with Dora and Diego*. New York: Simon & Schuster Audio.

Raffi. (1987). *Shake my sillies out*. New York: Random House.

Reid, M. (1990). *The button box*. New York: Puffin Unicorn.

Rockwell, A. (2001). *Welcome to kindergarten*. New York: Scholastic.

Rockwell, A., & Rockwell, H. (1987). *The first snowfall*. New York: Simon & Schuster.

Rogers, F. (1996). *Making friends*. New York: Penguin Group.

Sharmat. (1980). *Gregory the terrible eater*. New York: Scholastic.

Shaw, C. (1988). *Sometimes it looked like spilt milk*. New York: Harper.

Slate, J. (2002). *Miss Bindergarten celebrates the 100th day of school*. New York: Penguin Group.

Stutson, C. (2005). *Mamma loves you*. New York: Scholastic.

Tafuri, N. (1991). *Have you seen my duckling?* New York: HarperCollins.

Tafuri, N. (2003). *You are special little one*. New York: Scholastic.

Wells, R. (2000). *Timothy goes to school*. New York: Penguin Putnam Books for Young Readers.

Wyeth, S. (2005). *Something beautiful*. New York: Random House.

Children's Music

Devareaux Institute. *Songs of resilience*. Retrieved July 1, 2009, from http://www.kaplanco.com

Grammer, R. *Hello world!* Retrieved July 1, 2009, from http://www.redgrammer.com

Jenkins, E. *Sharing cultures with Ella Jenkins*. Retrieved August 21, 2009 from http://www.folkways.si.edu

Putumayo Kids. *World playground: A musical adventure for kids*. Retrieved July 1, 2009, from http://www.putumayokids.com

Zanes, D. ¡*Nueva York!* Retrieved July 1, 2009, from http://www.danzanes.com

FAMILY CALENDAR

NOTE TO TEACHERS: The letter below could be sent home with the monthly calendar on the following pages. Write in the dates for the month and personalize with important events, field trips, opportunities to volunteer, or any other reminders you need to give to families.

****

Dear Family,

Each month, you will receive a calendar that contains suggestions for activities you can do with your child that will help him or her meet kindergarten standards. The idea of the calendar is to do an activity with your child each day. In a year, you will have done 365 things to help your child learn! The activities will help your child be even more successful in kindergarten.

Research tells us that reading to children is one of the best ways to help them learn. Reading books will help your child learn to read, write, understand words and sentences, build vocabulary, and learn general knowledge that will help them in all areas of learning. Occasionally, point out the words in the books as you read them aloud. If possible, visit your local library where you can borrow books, music CDs, and other materials.

Talking and having enjoyable conversations with your child is also very important. Talk about what you are doing. Name things you see and use descriptive words to help your child learn new words. Do simple chores as you talk or sing together. Helping your child build a good vocabulary is a wonderful way to help her or him learn and is important to becoming a good reader. Let your child know that it's OK to make mistakes. Mistakes can help us learn. The important thing is to try. Praise your child for his or her efforts and let your child know that he or she is loved.

The early years are also the time to begin good health practices. Help your child learn to enjoy healthy foods by offering healthy food choices. This is also the time to make sure they get some playful activity and exercise each day, including walking, riding a bike, and just having fun playing.

The ideas presented on the calendar are very short in order to fit in the small space provided. The last week of the month provides a longer suggestion for the entire week. Feel free to interpret and adapt activities to fit your family. It may not be convenient to do each activity on the day it is mentioned. You can just do another activity or do it at a later time. Occasionally there will be questions to explore together or topics you can discuss. What is most important is to enjoy spending time together—read together, write together, exercise together, share healthy meals together, play together, and laugh together! Share your interests and things you find beautiful. Help your child see the wonder and beauty in each season and in the world around them.

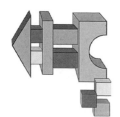

August

Looking forward to Kindergarten

Sunday	Monday	Tuesday	Wednesday	Thursday	Friday	Saturday
Read a book together about starting school	Play "I Spy" outside	Practice saying your address and phone number	Write your name beginning with a capital letter	Express wonder	Share stories from your early school days with your child	When is your birthday?
Read aloud and giggle	Explore something new	Express wonder at something beautiful outside	Talk about what you did today	What rhymes with pig?	Practice crossing the street together	Clean your child's room together
Read a book together with interesting facts	Make patterns, such as shoe/sock/shoe	Practice snapping and zipping	Check your child's immunization record	What words begin with an s like sun?	Find shapes in clouds	Play in water outside
Read aloud a book about going to school	Count to 10 then backward to one	Play with your shadow; what makes shadows?	Which is heavier, a spoon or a pan?	Count 10 things outside	Draw a cat. Write cat	Find summer beauty
Talk about how fun it can be to go to school and how fun it is to learn new things. Read books about starting school such as *Clifford's First School Day* by N. Bridwell and *Corduroy Goes to School* by D. Freeman						

Fun books: *The Kissing Hand* by A. Penn   *Welcome to Kindergarten* by A. Rockwell

NAEYC Web site: http://www.naeyc.org/families (Check out the *Early Years Are Learning Years* article "Helping Your Child Start School")

September

Sunday	Monday	Tuesday	Wednesday	Thursday	Friday	Saturday
Share a book with real facts	Start a growth chart with your child's height	Draw pictures with squares and circles	Read the numbers on a clock	Clap and say each sound in your name	Learn something new with your child	Throw small balls into a basket together
Read with a flashlight together	Play something new with your child	Use your imagination	Try a new art material together	Make up a silly song with your child	Line up toys by size together	Walk outside and look for numbers together
Read together on the floor	Practice your phone number with your child	Solve a problem together	Create something new with your child	Practice saying your address together	What do puppies grow up to be?	Play outside: is the wind blowing?
Read something new together	Sing a song from your childhood or culture	Express your joy	Pretend together	Make patterns (spoon, fork, spoon, fork)	Write "I love you!"	Invent a new sandwich together

Talk about ways to be a good friend: Sharing, being kind, saying nice things to each other, and asking what your friend would like to play.

Fun books: *All by Myself* by Aliki *Fish Eyes: A Book You Can Count On* by L. Ehlert

Parents as Teachers Web site: http://www.parentsasteachers.org

October

Sunday	Monday	Tuesday	Wednesday	Thursday	Friday	Saturday
Make up a new ending for a story together	Point out the front and back covers of books	Try making a foil boat with your child	Point out months on a calendar	What rhymes with tree?	Feel and talk about the sun's warmth	Watch ice melt together
Talk about the beginning, middle, and end of a book	Say hello in Spanish, "Hola"	Say goodbye in Spanish, "Adios"	Count in Spanish uno, dos, tres	Count *uno, dos, tres, quatro, cinco*	Find red (*rojo* in Spanish)	Say thank you in Spanish, "Gracias"
Enjoy reading a book outside together	Be curious, "I wonder what ____"	Gaze at clouds together	How do pumpkins grow?	How do apples grow?	Write words that rhyme with *fall*	Eat fresh fruits and vegetables together
Read a book about animals together	Predict together what will float in the tub	Find and name shapes in your home	Talk about changes in the season	Try walking forward and sideways with your child	Cut out circle shapes from paper together	Toast pumpkin seeds together

Encourage your child to wonder and appreciate the beauty of the world around her or him.
Consider taking a trip to a park, pumpkin patch, apple orchard, zoo, or even the library and talk about how amazing living things are!

Fun books: *Nuts to You* by L. Ehlert   *Circles, Triangles, and Squares* by T. Hoban

Sesame Street Web site: http://www.sesameworkshop.org

November

Sunday	Monday	Tuesday	Wednesday	Thursday	Friday	Saturday
Point out living things in a picture book	Write "I can play."	Play with magnetic letters together	Sing the ABC song with your child	Practice tying shoes together	Keep track of temperature outside with your child	Take a walk outside together
Read a nature book together	Find blue (azul in Spanish)	How are apples and pumpkins alike?	How are apples and pumpkins different?	What animal names start like yours?	What do animals need to live?	Look for living things outside together
Point out words on the cover of a book	Make a Thanksgiving card together	Find things that start with n	Talk about your family's culture and traditions	Write "thank you" (gracias in Spanish)	Practice address and phone number with your child	Make a favorite family recipe together
Read a Thanksgiving book together	Tell a story from your childhood	Make name cards for your family with your child	List what you are thankful for together	Give thanks! Gracias!	Count your blessings together	Count your fingers and toes together

During the last week of this month, talk about what makes your child special, including his or her name. Frequently practice writing his or her name with a capital letter first, followed by lowercase letters.

Fun books: *Over the River and Through the Woods* by M. Engelbreit   *Anamalia* by G. Base

Berit's Best Sites for Children Web site: http://www.beritsbest.com

127

December

Sunday	Monday	Tuesday	Wednesday	Thursday	Friday	Saturday
Read a science-related book together	Learn a new song with your child	Measure with a ruler together	Taste something new with your child	Listen to your favorite music together	Draw a dog; write *dog*	Recycle old clothes by donating them
Read an ABC book together	How can we take care of the earth?	Use your eyes and ears to observe together	Talk about how two things are similar	Talk about how two things are different	Make a card for a family member with your child	Use a thermometer to check temperature
Read a winter book aloud	Recycle your newspaper together	Reuse the backside of paper you have used	Find rhymes for your names	Predict together what will sink in the tub	Make a card for a friend with your child	Donate food to those in need together
Read a holiday book together	Find green (*verde* in Spanish)	Discuss differences between wants and needs	Why do we need water? How can we save it?	Share stories of your ancestors and relatives	Exercise together; do 10 sit-ups	Sing a favorite song together
Write New Year's resolutions together, such as *read a book and spend some time together every night in the new year.*						

Fun books: *Annie and the Wild Animals* by J. Brett   *The First Snowfall* by A. Rockwell

Scholastic Web site: http://www.scholastic.com/parents

128

January

Sunday	Monday	Tuesday	Wednesday	Thursday	Friday	Saturday
Snuggle and read with your child	Find white (*blanco* in Spanish)	Mark your child's height on a growth chart	Do 10 touch-your-toes together	Make a pattern (red, blue—red, red, blue)	Count out toys as first, second, third . . .	Find winter beauty together
Read aloud and stretch	Make it a habit to wash hands before eating	Prepare a healthy snack together	Brush your teeth; visit the dentist	Count doors and windows in your home together	Sing rhyming songs with your child	Be rockets: 10-9-8-7-6-5-4-3-2-1 blastoff!
Read a favorite book together	What food starts like your names?	Count 20 objects together	Practice tying shoes with your child	Help your child set the table and count the plates	Practice your phone number with your child	Point out and read signs in the grocery store
Read words on cereal boxes	Ask what we have more of, toes or ears?	Practice your address with your child	Talk about how to call 911 in case of emergency	What does a firefighter do?	What does a police officer do?	Throw folded socks into a basket together

Establish healthy eating and exercising habits with your child. Talk about safety issues, including not going anywhere with a stranger. Make a plan and practice what to do in case of fire: First, get out of your home safely then talk about where to go for help once outside.

Fun books: *Eating the Alphabet* by L. Ehlert   *My Opposites/Mis Opuestos* by R. Emberly

Kids Health Web site: http://kidshealth.org

February

Sunday	Monday	Tuesday	Wednesday	Thursday	Friday	Saturday
Read a counting book together	Can you see your shadow?	Do 10 stretches together	Row as you sing "Row, Row, Row Your Boat"	Say thank you in Spanish, "Gracias"	Practice cutting shapes with scissors	Play a board game together
Read a rhyming book aloud	Make heart patterns together	Send "I love you" notes	Do 10 touch-your-toes with your child	Clap and say "Hap-py Val-en-tines Day"	Write your names in hearts	Write "I love you!" on heart shapes for each other
Retell the story of the Three Bears	Draw a rectangle and triangle with your child	Find purple (púrpura in Spanish)	Add 2 spoons + 2 spoons = 4 spoons	Walk on a line of tape or yarn together	Count to 30 with your child	Move to slow and fast music together
Read a funny book together	Try skipping with your child	Hop on one foot together	Count chairs in your home with your child	What words begin with a b like ball?	Count by 10s to 50 (10-20-30-40-50)	Enjoy playing catch with a ball together

Make a different pattern every day, such as red toy, blue toy—red toy, blue toy, *or* spoon, spoon, cup—spoon, spoon, cup, and ask your child to repeat the pattern.

Fun books: *From Head to Toe* by E. Carle   *Shake My Sillies Out* by Raffi

Mister Rogers Neighborhood Web site: http://www.fci.org

March

Sunday	Monday	Tuesday	Wednesday	Thursday	Friday	Saturday
Ask your child to turn pages as you read aloud	Write your first and last name	Do 10 jumping jacks together	Sort toys by color with your child	Talk about where our light comes from	Count to 40 together	Jump like kangaroos
Read a favorite book together	Practice zipping with your child	Help your child write words rhyming with *cat*	Count pennies with your child	Practice skipping together	Count to 100 by 10s (10–20–30–40 . . .)	Make a castle with blocks
Read a book about friends	Find yellow (*amarillo* in Spanish)	Help your child practice tying shoes	Add 5 pennies + 5 pennies = 10 pennies	Count backwards from 10 together	Make a paper fan with your child	Celebrate spring!
Draw something you read about together	Practice tying shoes with your child	What rhymes with *can?*	Play with magnetic letters together	Practice snapping and buttoning with your child	Play matching games	Write and draw with sidewalk chalk together

Get a set of magnetic letters to put on your refrigerator or keep on a cookie sheet.
Encourage your child to write his or her name and simple words each week.

Fun books: *My Hands* by Aliki   *What Will I Do If I Can't Tie My Shoe?* by H. Kilgras

PBS Web site: http://www.pbskids.org

April

Sunday	Monday	Tuesday	Wednesday	Thursday	Friday	Saturday
Read a colorful book together	Paint a picture	Listen to music in the car	Write the word *ten*; count 10 things	Write words that rhyme with *dog*	Feel the wind and sing outside	Count a dozen (12) eggs or other objects
Discuss what an author is	Find pink (*rosa* in Spanish)	Cut circles together	Count to 50	Practice tying shoes	Draw with sidewalk chalk together	Sing while dusting
Talk about what an illustrator is	Look in a mirror, draw your faces together	Look in a mirror, draw your bodies together	Count by fives to 25 (5-10-15-20-25)	Have fun humming, make up a song	Count objects: first, second, third . . .	Bounce a ball
Discuss pictures in a book	Subtract two toys from four toys (4 – 2 = 2)	Practice writing your first and last name	Recycle newspapers	Make patterns with three colors	Make music on pots and pans and other instruments	Paint or draw outside

Put together an art/writing box with washable markers, crayons, pencils, and plain paper to promote creativity. Help your child decorate the box!

Fun Books: *You Are Special Little One* by N. Tafuri   *All the Colors of the Earth* by S. Hamanaka

Teaching Tolerance Web site: http://www.tolerance.org/parents

May

Sunday	Monday	Tuesday	Wednesday	Thursday	Friday	Saturday
Read together in a cozy place	Gallop like ponies; hop like frogs	Do the Twist with your child	Sort socks together	Sing something new together	Find rhymes for your names	Take a walk and find things near and far with your child
Read aloud with a stuffed animal	Find gray (*gris* in Spanish)	Dance or move to the beat of music together	Practice throwing a ball with your child	Compare and name a penny, nickel, and dime	Practice tying shoes with your child	Look for birds and nests together
Read about overcoming fears together	What makes you fearful? Happy?	Practice telling time on a clock with your child	Twirl, clap, twirl, clap together	Subtract three spoons from six spoons (6 - 3 = 3)	Set up a playhouse together	Cut fruit in half and talk about $\frac{1}{2}$
Read aloud then share a hug with your child	Measure with a shoe together	Write words that rhyme with *pig*	What words start like your name?	Enjoy rich conversations with your child	Play dress-up together	Plant seeds with your child

Every day this week, play with rhymes. Ask your child to find words that rhyme with his or her name and find words that begin with the same sound.

Fun books: *Amazing Grace* by C. Binch and M. Hoffman   *Count* by D. Fleming
Sesame Street for Parents Web site: http://www.sesameworkshop.org/parents

June

Sunday	Monday	Tuesday	Wednesday	Thursday	Friday	Saturday
Read a book about families together	Spend time together cleaning your child's room	Walk in the neighborhood hand-in-hand	Talk about what to do in case of fire	Share family photos with your child	Fold clothes together	Play a family game
Read about another country	Make up silly words that rhyme, such as "rilly" and "tilly"	Write the word *five* Count five things	Talk about when you were in kindergarten	Cut people pictures from magazines together	Share what you played as a child	Have lunch outside together
Talk about characters in books you read	Show appreciation for each other	Sing while setting the table together	Find numbers in a newspaper or magazine	Dust tables; name other things that start with *t*	Be a good neighbor	Talk as you work outside
Make an *All About Me & My Family* book	Count by fives to 50 (5-10-15-20-25 . . .)	Make patterns with circles and squares together	Talk about accepting differences with your child	Practice saying "please" and "thank you"	Write a letter to a friend or relative with your child	Make a treasure map together

Talk about how special families are and how each member of the family can contribute and help each other to be happy. Give your child a simple job, such as dusting with an old sock.

Fun books: *Families Are Different* by N. Pellegrini   *A Color of His Own* by L. Lioni
Jan Brett Web site: http://www.janbrett.com

July

Sunday	Monday	Tuesday	Wednesday	Thursday	Friday	Saturday
Read under a tree together	What is the opposite of *up*?	Count letters in your first and last names		Draw a pattern (red, red, blue—red, red, blue)	Smile! What rhymes with smile?	Look for living things outside together
Find rhymes for book character names	Where does milk come from? Eggs?	Subtract four toys from nine toys (9 − 4 = 5)	Count by twos to 10 (2-4-6-3-10)	What does a waiter do?	List ways your child is special	Enjoy a healthy treat together
Read a book about a real person	Find things that end with *t*	Freeze juice in ice cube trays	Play restaurant with your child	What is the opposite of *fast*?	Write the word *six* Count six things	Do sink and float activities outside together
Find favorite letters in a book together	Sign your names on a card	What is the opposite of *hot*?	Skip together	Talk about what happened *yesterday*	Sort coins (pennies, nickels, dimes)	Find cubes and other shapes outside together
			Practice tying shoes with your child			

Set up a cozy reading area where your child can cuddle up and read. Use pillows, a beanbag chair, or a large stuffed animal and a basket of books. Build vocabulary by reading to your child, talking as you do activities together and pointing out objects you see.

Fun books: *Families* by A. Morris   *Goodnight Moon, Buenas Noches Luna* by M. Wise Brown

Educational Games Web site: http://www.starfall.com

August

Sunday	Monday	Tuesday	Wednesday	Thursday	Friday	Saturday
Read about a new place together	Draw a house	Build a home with blocks	Buy school supplies	Write your child's name on school supplies	Pack a backpack for school	Plan a picnic
Read a book together about making friends	Make a list of school supplies you need	Put letter magnets in ABC order	Write words that rhyme with *cat*	Draw a picture of your school	Find things that end with *s*	Ride a bike or take a walk
Ask your child to read to you	What is a river?	What is your town's name? Build a town with blocks	Count by twos to 20 (2–4–6–8–10 . . .)	What do living things need?	Eat fresh vegetables	Take a walk, talk, and read signs
Read a book together about starting school	Write the ABCs	Play school	Add 3 spoons + 5 spoons = 8 spoons	Make a map of your neighborhood	Cut grass with a child's scissors	Check your child's height on your growth chart

Encourage your child to read simple books to you often.

Write short sentences, stories, or letters to friends and relatives together and then read them.

Fun Books: *Will I Have a Friend?* by M. Cohen   *Timothy Goes to School* by R. Wells

Suessville Web site: http://www.seussville.com

Label Lemur

Lemur del la Etiqueta

Make a name badge children can wear when it's their turn to label something around the room. See Chapter 2 for more details. The name badge can be double-sided including both English and Spanish. Attaching to cardstock and laminating will provide more durability. Add ribbon or yarn to make it easy for children to put it on and take it off themselves.

References

Anderson, R., Hiebert, E., Scott, J., & Wilkinson, I. A. G. (1985). *Becoming a nation of readers: The report of the commission on reading*. Champaign, IL: University of Illinois, Center for the Study of Reading; Washington, DC: National Institute of Education.

Arndt, J., & McGuire-Schwartz, M. E. (2008). Early childhood school success: Recognizing families as integral partners. *Childhood Education, 84*(5), 281.

Berk, L., & Winsler, A. (1996). *Scaffolding children's learning: Vygosky and early childhood education.* Washington, DC: National Association for the Education of Young Children.

Bodrova, E., & Leong, D. (1996). *Tools of the mind.* Columbus, OH: Prentice Hall.

Bronson, M. (2006). Developing social and emotional competence. In D. Gullo (Ed.), *K Today* (pp. 47–56). Washington, DC: National Association for the Education of Young Children.

Burns, S., Griffin, P., & Snow, C. (1999). *Starting out right: A guide to promoting children's reading success.* Washington, DC: National Academies Press. Retrieved July 1, 2009, from http://books.nap.edu/openbook.php?record_id=6014 &page=R1

Cadwell, L. (2008). Thinking about the environment: Inspirations from the Reggio approach. In A. Gordon & K. Brown (Eds.), *Beginnings and beyond* (pp. 373–374). Clifton Park, NY: Thomson Delmar.

Carson, R. (1965). *The sense of wonder.* New York: Harper & Row.

Copple, C., & Bredekamp, S. (Ed.). (2009). *Developmentally appropriate practice in early childhood programs, serving children from birth through age 8.* Washington, DC: National Association for the Education of Young Children.

Curtis, D., & Carter, M. (2003). *Designs for living and learning: Transforming early childhood environments.* St. Paul, MN: Redleaf Press.

Dickinson, D., & Neuman, S. (Eds.). (2007). *The handbook of early literacy research* (Vol. 2). New York: Guilford.

Dodge, D., Colker, L., & Heroman, C. (2002). *The creative curriculum for preschool,* (4th ed.). Washington, DC: Teaching Strategies.

Elicker, J. (2000). *Full-day kindergarten: Exploring the research.* Bloomington, IN: Phi Delta Kappa International.

Epstein, A. (2007). *The intentional teacher.* Washington, DC: National Association for the Education of Young Children.

Fisher, B. (1998). *Joyful learning in kindergarten.* Portsmouth, NH: Heinemann.

Fisher, B., & Medvic, E. F. (2000). *Perspectives on shared reading: Planning and practice.* Portsmouth, NH: Heinemann.

Froebel, F. (1887). *The education of man.* New York: Appleton & Company.

Fulghum, R. (1988). *All I really needed to know I learned in kindergarten.* New York: Random House.

Good, L. (2009). *Teaching and learning with digital photography.* Thousand Oaks, CA: Corwin.

Goodman, J., & Balamore, U. (2003). *Teaching goodness: Engaging the moral and academic promise of young children.* Boston, MA: Allyn & Bacon.

Gullo, D. (Ed.). (2006). *K today: Teaching and learning in the kindergarten year.* Washington, DC: National Association for the Education of Young Children.

Hart, B., & Risley, T. (2003). The early catastrophe. *Education Review, 17*(1), 110–18.

Heidemann, S., & Hewitt, D. (2010). *Play: The pathway from theory to practice* (Rev. ed.). St. Paul, MN: Redleaf Press.

Heroman, C., & Copple, C. (2006). Teaching in the kindergarten year. In D. Gullo (Ed.), *K today: Teaching and learning in the kindergarten year* (pp. 59–72). Washington, DC: National Association for the Education of Young Children.

Hyson, M. (2004). *The emotional development of young children: Building an emotion-centered curriculum.* New York: Teacher's College Press.

Hyson, M. (2008). *Enthusiastic and engaged: Strengthening young children's positive approaches to learning.* New York: Teachers College Press.

Jacobs, G., & Crowley, K. (2007). *Play, projects, and preschool standards: Nurturing children's sense of wonder and joy in learning.* Thousand Oaks, CA: Corwin.

Jalongo, M. R., & Isenberg, J. P. (2006). Creative expression and thought in kindergarten. In D. Gullo (Ed.), *K today: Teaching and learning in the kindergarten year* (pp. 116–126). Washington, DC: National Association for the Education of Young Children.

Kagan, S. L., & Kauerz, K. (2006). Making the most of kindergarten: Trends and policy issues. In D. Gullo (Ed.), *K Today* (pp. 161–170). Washington, DC: National Association for the Education of Young Children.

Kaiser, B., & Rasminsky, J. (2003). *Challenging behavior in young children: Understanding, preventing, and responding effectively.* Boston, MA: Allyn & Bacon.

Katz, L. (2007). Viewpoint: Standards of experience. *Young Children, 62*(3), 94–95.

Knopf, H., & Swick, K. (2008). Using our understanding of families to strengthen family involvement. *Early Childhood Education Journal, 35*(5), 419–427.

Levin, D., & Kilbourne, J. (2008). *So sexy so soon: The new sexualized childhood and what parents can do to protect their kids.* New York: Random House.

National Association of State Specialists in State Departments of Education. (2000). *Still unacceptable trends in kindergarten entry and placement.* Retrieved July 1, 2009, from http://208.118.177.216/about/positions/pdf/Psunacc.pdf

National Council of Teachers of Mathematics and the National Association for the Education of Young Children. (2002). *Early childhood mathematics: Promoting good beginnings* (Position Statement). Washington, DC; National Association for the Education of Young Children. Retrieved July 1, 2009 from http://www.naeyc.org/positionstatements/mathematics

National Council for the Social Studies. (2008). *Curriculum standards for social studies, update draft.* Retrieved July 1, 2009, from http://www.socialstudies.org/standards

National Governors Association. (2005). *Building the foundation for bright futures: The final report of the NGA task force on school readiness.* Retrieved July 1, 2009, from http://www.nga.org/Files/pdf/0501TaskForceReadiness.pdf

Nelson, R. F. (2000). Which is the best kindergarten? *Principal, 79*(5), 38–41.

Neuman, S. B., Copple, C., & Bredekamp, S. (2000). *Learning to read and write: Developmentally appropriate practices for young children.* Washington, DC: National Association for the Education of Young Children.

Pianta, R., LaParo, K., & Hamre, B. (2008). *The classroom assessment scoring system (CLASS) manual.* Baltimore, MD: Brooks.

Pianta, R., & Kraft-Sayer, M. (2003). *Successful kindergarten transition: Your guide to connecting children, families and schools.* Baltimore, MD: Brookes Publishing.

Porch, S. (2002). *Full day kindergarten.* Arlington, VA: Educational Research Service.

Sanders, S. (2002). *Active for life: Developmentally appropriate movement programs for young children.* Washington, DC: National Association for the Education of Young Children.

Sanders, S. (2006). Physical education in kindergarten. In D. Gullo (Ed.), *K today: Teaching and learning in the kindergarten year* (pp. 127–137). Washington, DC: National Association for the Education of Young Children.

Seefeldt, C. (2005). *How to work with standards in early childhood classrooms.* New York: Teachers College Press.

Shonkoff, J., & Phillips, D. (Eds.). (2000). *From neurons to neighborhoods: The science of early childhood development.* Committee on Integrating the Science of Early Childhood Development, National Research Council and Institute of Medicine: Washington, DC: National Academy Press. Retrieved July 1, 2009, from http://www.nap.edu

Snow, C., Griffin, P., & Burns, S. (Eds.). (2005). *Knowledge to support the teaching of reading.* Hoboken, NJ: John Wiley.

Strickland, D., & Ayers, S. (2007). *Literacy leadership in early childhood: The essential guide.* New York: Teacher's College Press.

Tomlinson, H. B. (2009). Developmentally appropriate practice in the kindergarten year. In C. Copple & S. Bredekamp (Eds.), *Developmentally appropriate practice in early childhood programs: Serving children from birth through age 8* (pp. 187–216). Washington, DC: National Association for the Education of Young Children.

Topal, C. W., & Gandini, L. (1999). *Beautiful stuff: Learning with found materials.* New York: Sterling.

Vecchiotti, S. (2001). *Kindergarten: The overlooked school year.* New York: Foundation for Child Development. (ERIC Document Reproduction Service No. ED458948).

Vygotsky, L. S. (1978). *Mind in Society: The development of higher mental processes* (M. Cole, V. John-Steiner, S. Scribner, & E. Souberman, Eds. & Trans.). Cambridge, MA: Harvard University Press.

Wenner, M. (2009) The serious need for play. *Scientific American Mind, 20*(1), 22–29.

Wurm, J. (2005). *Working in the Reggio way: A beginners guide for American teachers.* St. Paul, MN: Redleaf Press.

Suggested Readings

Andrews, A. (2002). *Little kids—powerful problem solvers.* Portsmouth, NH: Heinemann.

Chalufour, I., & Worth, K. (2003). *Discovering nature with young children.* St. Paul, MN: Redleaf Press.

Gartrell, D. (2004). *The power of guidance: Teaching social emotional skills in early childhood classrooms.* Clifton Park: NY: Thompson Delmar Learning; Washington, DC: NAEYC.

Meier, D. (2004). *The young child's memory for words: Developing first and second language and literacy.* Washington, DC: NAEYC.

Teaching Strategies. (2005, 2006). *The Creative Curriculum® study starters: A step-by-step guide to project-based investigations in science and social studies.* (Teacher's Guide; Vol. 1: Boxes, Rocks, Ants, Clothes, Flowers, Buildings, Balls; Vol. 2: Chairs and Things to Sit On, Wheels, Water Pipes, Trash & Garbage, Shadows, Exercise). Washington, DC: Author.

Thompson, S. (2005). *Children as illustrators: Making meaning through art and language.* Washington, DC: NAEYC.

Walmsley, B., & Wing, D. (2004). *Welcome to kindergarten.* Portsmouth, NH: Heinemann.

Index

CORWIN
A SAGE Company

The Corwin logo—a raven striding across an open book—represents the union of courage and learning. Corwin is committed to improving education for all learners by publishing books and other professional development resources for those serving the field of PreK–12 education. By providing practical, hands-on materials, Corwin continues to carry out the promise of its motto: **"Helping Educators Do Their Work Better."**

Founded in 1926, the National Association for the Education of Young Children (NAEYC) is the world's largest organization working on behalf of young children, with nearly 90,000 members, a national network of more than 300 local, state, and regional Affiliates, and a growing global alliance of like-minded organizations. NAEYC's mission is to serve and act on behalf of the needs, rights, and well-being of all young children, birth to age 8, with primary focus on providing educational and developmental services and resources to practitioners working in early childhood education, teacher-educators, and students preparing for a career in the field.

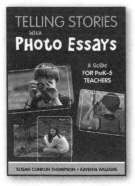

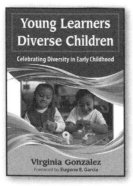